T0334106

Musicians' Migratory Patterns

Musicians' Migratory Patterns: American-Mexican Border Lands considers the works and ideologies of an array of American-based, immigrant Mexican musicians. It asserts their immigrant status as a central force in nourishing, informing, and propelling musical and artistic concerns, uncovering pure and fresh forms of expression that broaden the multicultural map of Mexico. The text guides readers in appreciation of the aesthetic and technical achievements of original works and innovative performances, with artistic and pedagogical implications that frame a vivid picture of the contemporary Mexican as immigrant creator in the United States.

The ongoing displacement of Mexicans into the United States impacts not only American economic conditions but the country's social, cultural, and intellectual configurations as well. Artistic and academic voices shape and enrich the multicultural diversity of both countries, as immigrant Mexican artists and their musics prove instrumental to the forming of a self-critical society compelled to value and embrace its diversity. Despite conflicting political reactions on this complex subject of legal and illegal immigration, undeniable is the influence of Mexican musical expressions in the United States and Mexico, at the border and beyond.

Mauricio Rodríguez has taught at American universities and also in Spain. He is an artistic fellow of the National Endowment for the Arts of Mexico.

CMS Cultural Expressions in Music
Series Editor: Franco Sciannameo
Carnegie Mellon University

Created in 2009, *Cultural Expressions in Music* began as a series of monographs that sought to promote and share the diversity of perspectives, cultures, experiences, philosophies, and contributions of The College Music Society's membership and the music community at large. The volumes published under this rubric follow the tenets of geo-musicology, an interdisciplinary outreach of recent coinage, which integrates musical expression, geo-political thinking, and migratory movement of musicians, musical genres, styles, repertoire, and practices. The monographs and edited collections in the series urge readers worldwide to reflect, musically and culturally, upon one of the most pressing issues of our time: immigration.

Musicians' Migratory Patterns
American-Mexican Border Lands
Edited by Mauricio Rodriguez

Musicians' Migratory Patterns
The African Drum as Symbol in Early America
Christopher Johnson

Musicians' Migratory Patterns
The Adriatic Coasts
Edited by Franco Sciannameo

Musicians' Migratory Patterns

American-Mexican Border Lands

Edited by
Mauricio Rodríguez

Routledge
Taylor & Francis Group

NEW YORK AND LONDON

First published 2020
by Routledge
52 Vanderbilt Avenue, New York, NY 10017

and by Routledge
2 Park Square, Milton Park, Abingdon, Oxon, OX14 4RN

Routledge is an imprint of the Taylor & Francis Group, an informa business

© 2020 Taylor & Francis

The rights of Mauricio Rodríguez to be identified as the author of the editorial material, and of the authors for their individual chapters, has been asserted in accordance with sections 77 and 78 of the Copyright, Designs and Patents Act 1988.

Trademark notice: Product or corporate names may be trademarks or registered trademarks, and are used only for identification and explanation without intent to infringe.

Library of Congress Cataloging-in-Publication Data
Names: Rodríguez, Mauricio, editor.
Title: Musicians' migratory patterns : American-Mexican border
   lands / edited by Mauricio Rodriguez.
Description: New York : Routledge, 2020. | Series: CMS cultural
   expressions in music | Includes bibliographical references and
   index.
Identifiers: LCCN 2020003107 (print) | LCCN 2020003108
   (ebook) | ISBN 9781138325340 (hardback) | ISBN
   9780367498160 (paperback) | ISBN 9780429450440
   (ebook)
Subjects: LCSH: Mexicans—United States—Music—History and
   criticism. | Music—United States—History and criticism.
   | Music—Mexico—History and criticism.
Classification: LCC ML199.9 .M87 2020 (print) | LCC ML199.9
   (ebook) | DDC 780.9/720973—dc23
LC record available at https://lccn.loc.gov/2020003107
LC ebook record available at https://lccn.loc.gov/2020003108

ISBN: 978-1-138-32534-0 (hbk)
ISBN: 978-0-367-49816-0 (pbk)
ISBN: 978-0-429-45044-0 (ebk)

Typeset in Times New Roman
by Apex Covantage, LLC

Contents

Preface

In Gabriel Pareyón's *Diccionario Enciclopédico de Música en México* (Universidad Panamericana, 2007), the phrase *Estados Unidos de América* appears 1,338 times. Pareyón's two-volume compendium totaling 1,134 pages is a paramount bibliographic recount of the lives and musical experiences of Mexican musicians and artists from pre-Columbian times to today. The artistic, academic, cultural, social, and economic ties of Mexican musicians to the United States cannot be simply understood by such a significant number; however, this mere statistical value no doubt informs us about the strong musical relationships between the two countries. This bonded relationship is somewhat obvious. Until the mid-19th century, the southwestern border of the United States was part of Mexico, so for musicians at the crossborder (and for the rest of the Mexican people too) the mobility between the two countries has been always a natural transit, a fluid geographical displacement that is part of thousands of Mexican (and American) lives.

The idea for this collection of essays finds its origin in 2017, when I organized the first panel discussion on "Contemporary Mexican Music and Immigration". This panel took place at the Center of Latin American Studies (CLAS) at Stanford University and was supported by the General Mexican Consulate in San Jose, which hosted Mexican composers Guillermo Galindo, Ivan Naranjo, Pablo Rubio, and me. This was a public presentation to discuss the extent our immigration perspective informed, inspired, and nourished our creative expression as Mexican composers in the United States. Based on that first discussion, in 2018 I gave a lecture in San Antonio, Texas at the National Conference of the College Music Society, entitled "Composition from the Outside: Aesthetic Concerns and Artistic Works by Immigrant Mexican Composers". This presentation discussed the immigrant status of composers as catalyst for music creation. I was fortunate to have in my audience Professor Franco Sciannameo, editor of the College Music Society's series *Cultural Expressions in Music*. A conversation afterwards about the plight of immigrant, exiled, and expatriate Mexican composers to the United

States outlined the workings for a tangible course toward the present collection of essays.

From the outset of this project, I primarily wanted to depict some of the current artistic and researching voices that, with their everyday work, shape and enrich the multicultural diversity of both countries. Therefore, the chapters comprising this book frame research work reflecting contemporary musical expressions—expressions that are also very personal, almost intimate, to their respective authors. The writing of the essays favors a "first-person" (rather experiential) approach, where the musicological relevance of the covered subjects is evidenced just in the "aftertaste" of the readings. This book does not follow any of the well-established paths when discussing Mexican music in the United States, either as studies of musics whose Mexican roots have found their path into Americanized expressions (such as Tejano music, forms of Latin jazz, or more recently for instance, Border Fandango), or as texts on musics of folk origin played in the United States by Mexicans and their descendants who seek forging their identity in a foreign land. This book is less conventional in its approach; in fact, if there is a general concept that somewhat ties together most of the present essays, it is something that I loosely define as New Immigrant Mexican Music, and this collection is written with the research and experiences that directly (or indirectly) try to understand contemporary Mexican expressions at the border and beyond. The adjective "New" in this context should be understood in its literal meaning, including musics that are always new as the result of the emerging works of improvisation, experimentation, and listening. With that general disclaimer to the reader, a brief description of the contents of this book is in order.

The opening chapter is an original, rather immersive, ecoacoustics research by Álvaro G. Díaz Rodríguez that describes the soundscape at the American-Mexican cross-line between Tijuana and San Diego, California. Díaz Rodríguez approaches the subject matter with a "dimensional sonology" that informs us and lets us experience "how the border sounds". Beyond the sound of the walled beach (Figure 1.1) or the United States patrol helicopters hovering over the zone, the author strikes a chord with us when describing how the border has achieved a "new level of loudness", particularly at the Mexican side, due to the massive and increasing presence of "American Dream" seekers. Ultimately, though, all the sounding descriptions of this chapter are a comprehensive acoustic ecology that makes us appreciate the unique "sound novels" at the border and discover, through them, the particular characteristics of border societies and the spaces they inhabit.

The second chapter traces the origins of the digital art scene at the Tijuana–San Diego border. Rossana Lara Velázquez's essay discusses the overall aesthetics and rather political position of several multimedia, visual, and sound artists that are part of the cyberculture at the United States–Mexican border. Velázquez's essay argues that the production of art (and identities) promoted by digital culture movements at the frontier emerged and developed as a critical reflection of the border inequalities between the two countries. "Hacktivism" allowed artists at the turn of the 21st century to reflect and position themselves in relation to border experiences, "seeking to surpass and erase borderlines at times, or critically assuming and exposing them at others", she writes. Digital activist actions of those pioneers are still inspiring models for current artists, those seeking to interpret and express the border as a permanent conflicting multidimensional site.

Chapters 3 and 4 are inspiring and informative biographic recounts told by artists whose professional and academic work take place in bi-national settings. In the third chapter, Wilfrido Terrazas, a remarkable and extremely prolific Mexican musician, presents a condensed autobiography that intimately describes his artistic development and output on both sides of the border. His stimulating narrative vividly describes a very personal creative process and lets us see in him what he sees in other creators as "integral artists". Crossing "inner sonic borders", morphing often into compartmentalized music expressions, such as composition, improvisation, performance, and so on, is what Terrazas learned from his own experiential relation to the physical border. While actively crossing the border since his formation years as a trans-border musician, Terrazas came to understand that "crossing the border is the essence of it", and that the act of crossing is what permeates into his artistic work. Terrazas' essay is also significant for understanding the meaning of his original music concepts (such as "mobile temporality" and his creative "growth modules"); however, his touching narrative is probably the most rewarding offer to his readers; I am sure they will very likely enjoy as much as I did when reading: "Once upon a time, there were two kids who played the flute on either side of the border . . .".

In Chapter 4, Teresa Díaz de Cossio and Paul N. Roth continue Terrazas' autobiographical narrative with a current recount of their personal experiences as active actors of the artistic border scene. I find it appropriate here to let these authors present the idea of their text with the following thorough description:

[This] is a collaborative dialogue between two friends and colleagues from the graduate music program at UC San Diego: Teresa Díaz de Cossio (b. Newport Beach CA, raised Ensenada, 1987) and Paul N. Roth (b. Buffalo NY, 1983). Together we focus on experimentalist musical practice in Teresa's hometown of Ensenada, Baja California. We first detail a lineage of the scene's beginnings and developments, from the last quarter of the 20th century with pianist/composer/educator Ernesto

Rosas on through the multiple generations of musicians and frameworks for musical practice and aesthetics he sets in motion. To do so we draw from ethnographic work undertaken throughout 2019 in Ensenada, Tijuana, Mexico City, and San Diego. Second, we discuss Teresa's personal experience in and around these musical activities, including local particulars of the scene's most-recent large-scale iteration—the 2nd Festival de Música Nueva Ensenada (August 2019)—of which she was primary organizer. Ensenada as place is central to the unique ways these practices have emerged and prospered, and, for context, we provide a brief (but admittedly incomplete) introduction to the city. Within the frame of real-time dialogue and brevity, we don't fully explore the many salient issues related to music and migration that arise. We hope, however, this conversation encourages further reflection and discussion for our readers.

The last two chapters of the book revisit the idea approached in my paper presentation at the College Music Society's conference in 2017, talking about the work of Mexican composers based in the United States of America. In the fifth chapter, Turcios Ruiz discusses the piano work of Samuel Zyman, an established composer and scholar at the Juilliard School of Music. His essay offers a comprehensive description of the aesthetic and technical grounds of this Mexican creator, observing how his influences of Mexican and American music permeate in all his musical output. The essay concludes with an extensive analysis of a seminal work by Zyman, a piece of music that Ruiz has performed and recorded as part of his interpretative research to approach the music of the composer.

The closing chapter is my own tribute to the Mexican Orchestra, an artistic project originally conceived by Carlos Chávez in the 1930s but reconstituted 80 years later by a group of Mexican ethnomusicologists led by Rubén Luengas. The newly created POM (Pasatono Orquesta Mexicana) has become in recent years an active ensemble promoting folk, traditional, and new Mexican music in Mexico and the United States. My chapter concludes with the description of a collaborative project with POM, a piece of music that attempts both, honoring the indigenous music of Mexico and America with a contemporary reinterpretation, and showing my gratitude to the ensemble and its tireless efforts to diffuse Mexican music wherever they go.

Acknowledgments

I thank each and every one of the authors who contributed to this book. Within the length constraints of this short collection, it is not possible to give a complete view of the countless perspectives of the musical relationship between Mexico and the United States. However, the thorough research work of all the authors in this book no doubt gives a very informative view on the state of affairs at the border and beyond. While deeply thanking the presented authors, I also apologize to those not included here whose intellectual and artistic activities daily enrich the cultural landscape in both countries.

Last but not least, I sincerely thank Professor Franco Sciannameo for his supportive insights on the contents and structure of this publication: he is ultimately the propelling mind behind it.

Mauricio Rodríguez
December 2019
Palo Alto, California

1 Sound Through the Looking Glass

An Approach to the Dimensional Sonology on the Tijuana–San Diego Border

Álvaro G. Díaz Rodríguez

> First, there's the room you can see through the glass—that's just the same as our drawing room, only the things go the other way.
>
> *Through the Looking Glass*
> (Carroll, 1896: 15)

One Sunday last summer, I accompanied my girlfriend and a group of musician friends from the University of California San Diego (UCSD) to perform on the beach in San Diego, improvising with a group of Mexican musicians on the other side of the beach in Tijuana. These two beaches are divided only by the border wall (Figure 1.1). There were four musicians from UCSD and five musicians in the Bachelor of Music program at the Universidad Autónoma de Baja California (UABC). I was in charge of recording the "dialogue" between the two groups of musicians. There were a lot of people on the Mexican side of the beach. I was struck by the sounds captured from the other side of the wall of families having fun, of the bells of the *paleteros* and children yelling. On my side, the American side, the only sounds captured were of birds, waves, and wind. There weren't any people except the musicians and an immigration officer who was guarding the border from his big green and white truck. The difference in the sounds from the two sides was radical. A single barrier managed to divide the soundscape even though visually and geographically, it was the same sand, the same ocean, and the same sunset. From this arose my idea to investigate the different soundscapes emanating from one of the world's most studied borders in recent decades. Some questions arose: What sounds characterize and shape a city? Do sound borders exist? How can we identify a society from its soundscape?

In the specific case of the Tijuana–San Diego border, sociological and economic studies are not enough to understand the intricate panorama. A profound listening is required, a new way to recognize through listening

Figure 1.1 Border Wall, Tijuana–San Diego Beach

and analyzing the soundscape from distinct dimensions. In his book *Sonic Agency*, Brandon LaBelle says:

> Sound is political by extending or restricting the limits of the body, in the desires and needs announced in the cry, through the care and compassion listening may yield, and in acts of rupture and fragmentation, improvisation—the rapturous and violating noises that return us to the base materialism of bare life.
>
> (LaBelle, 2018: 6)

Here we will take some soundscapes as a guide to uncover the tangled border phenomenon between Tijuana and San Diego through the dimensionality that listening provokes.

Border and Location in Tijuana and San Diego

> Wandering up and down, and trying turn after turn,
> but always coming back to the house, do what she would.
>
> *Through the Looking Glass*
> (Carroll, 1896: 27)

We begin by looking for a definition that can help us to understand the new concept of border. The general idea is that a border is a division between two territories or two cultures. It is a real or imaginary boundary between two objects, the separation of two cultures often dissimilar, sometimes the same. The word border comes from the Latin *frons* or *frontis* which translates as "frontage" or "façade"; however, the connotation that the word has will vary in each situation. Silvia Ruzzi mentions that the border areas represent a space for interaction between cultures and, although they are identified as transnational places, this does not imply the loss of hegemony on the part of the subordinate indigenous culture nor the weakness of the nation state (Ruzzi, 2014: 110). And fittingly this interaction is what takes place at the Tijuana–San Diego border. While there is a physical wall, the cities complement each other at the same time that they intermingle and, on some occasions, repel and assault each other.

Defining Tijuana is a complex task as there is no single Tijuana. Geographically, socially, and chronologically, there are many different Tijuanas. Over the last few decades, we can find above all, in the words of Heriberto Yépez (Yépez, 2006: 13), a historical division. Before 2013, drug trafficking was actively positioned within Tijuana society and mired in a high rate of violence. After the *narcos*, another Tijuana took over when the multiple, almost countless homicides began to decline and a rebound started in the maquiladora industry. Depending on the study being carried out, Tijuana has a different definition. It's as if it tries to hide its face and show it only to those who have something to offer. Yépez likewise defined Tijuana in 2006 "as a woman who goes crazy, a woman who can't forget, uttering lies or insults, an exciting and terrible woman, a city that consumes and destroys itself" (Yépez, 2006: 13). Is it really such a mysterious city? Although Tijuana is created from a myth from which it still survives, this city reinvents itself from its inhabitants, some that arrive and others that leave although the majority never actually get out of Tijuana.

I believe that one needs to analyze the location of the border and the characteristics of each of the cities in order to understand the looking glass through which one can look at both sides of the border. Tijuana is located in the northwest of the Mexican Republic, joining in the north the county of San Diego, United States of America; in the west the Pacific Ocean; in the east the municipality of Tecate; and in the south the municipality of Rosarito. It comprises nine districts: El Centro—known as the historic zone, Otay Centenario, Playas de Tijuana, La Mesa, San Antonio de las Minas, Sánchez Taboada, Cerro Colorado, La Presa, and La Presa Rural. According to the 2015 census from the Instituto Nacional de Estadística y Geografía (INEGI, 2015), the population of Tijuana in 2015 was 1,641,570 of a total population of 3,348,898 in the state of Baja California.

Tijuana has also grown in recent years because many *paisanos*[1] have been deported and, due to insufficient funds to allow them to return to their own cities, have looked for a second chance in Tijuana. Some others coming from the center of the country have simply decided to migrate to the north without hope of crossing. They looked for a type of "Mexican dream", a place to work and send money to their families without the need to risk their lives crossing the border. The myths and realities of the illegal crossing as well as the hope for a better life have arrived in many corners of Mexico. So, some elect to work in a factory or be a merchant in a swap meet or other type of *changarro*.[2] As well in recent years, Tijuana has been inundated with caravans of migrants from Haiti and South America who, having been denied political asylum in the United States, have stayed in the city.

In 2016, some Haitians arrived in Tijuana with the aim of crossing the border. However, the changes in American politics regarding political asylum caused this group to stay in Tijuana, or in many other cases to be deported. Data provided by the Instituto Nacional de Migración (INM) and cited in the report from the Colegio de la Frontera Norte (COLEF) show that from April of 2017, close to 3,400 foreigners originating in Haiti stayed in Baja California: 75% in Tijuana and 25% in Mexicali (Albicker *et al.*, 2017: 16). In November of 2016, the shelters were at maximum capacity, and there was no immediate solution for such a large number of migrants. Fortunately, they were accepted by the Baja Californian community, and spontaneously began to work. The community built them houses and quickly gave them work permits. Many of them started to create a family with the residents of Tijuana, exchanging their longing to cross the border with the aim of getting work and creating a life in Tijuana.

This interracial mixture has also had a musical influence on Tijuana: the Haitijuana movement arose. This is a mix of Haitian sounds with border language, created in this city that gave them new citizenship (Antiguo cine Libertad, 2018). The first concert *Haitijuana* was given in the Cine Libertad on the 14th of April, 2018, and there was a sequel on the 22nd of September, 2018, encompassing rap rhythms with Haitian rhythms, mixing local words like "chingón", "raza", "jefita" and "guey" with other words in *kreyòl* (Espacio migrante, 2018).

Two years later, the story of massive migration to Tijuana continued. In July of 2019, the Instituto Nacional de Migración published a statement indicating that around 7,000 Central Americans were in Tijuana. Many were of Honduran origin, although there were also Guatemalans along with migrants from El Salvador and Belize (INM, 2019) who joined the Central American caravan formed on the 13th of October, 2018, by some Hondurans whose goal was to cross the border into the United States.

Among the main reasons these migrants left their countries were poverty and extreme violence as well as some natural disasters that they had lived through (COLEF, 2018). The truth is that, as Alberto Pradilla says in his book *Caravana: cómo el éxodo centroamericano salió de la clandestinidad*, the plan of this caravan on its arrival in Tijuana was clear up to this point, but now they faced a metal wall and many other invisible walls with the metal one being the smallest of them all (Pradilla, 2019: pos. 3430). When they arrived in Tijuana, these Central Americans could hear exclamations of support, but differently from the Haitians, they also heard many cries of indignation from the people of Tijuana at their arrival. The Central American voices mingled with the strong, rude accent of the northern locals. These were joined by the laughter and weeping of the Central Americans from the feeling of having arrived at the wall and seeing the other side through the bars in spite of the many risks and hardships.

On some occasions, they were silenced and frightened by the xenophobic cries of the many protestors who settled themselves at the border waiting for the return of these migrants, calling them criminals, murderers, and invaders. A few days later, everything got out of control. On the 25th of November, 2018, some desperate migrants tried to forcibly enter San Diego whereupon the border patrol launched tear gas. You could hear the sounds of tear gas, rubber bullets bursting, helicopters, police sirens, alarms, car horns, shouts, and whistles, and rallying cries from the Central Americans at the edge of El Chaparral.[3] It was a thunderous polyphony with the shouts of Mexican police in the middle (Euronews, 2018). A new loudness had reached the border. For many years, only the sound of the border patrol helicopter had been constantly heard; never before these other sounds.

According to a report from the University of Syracuse, from 2013 to 2018, there were 2,050 cases of political asylum heard in the immigration courts in San Diego, California, of which 26.5% were granted and 73.5% were rejected (TRACInmigration, 2018). These figures show the complexity of the relationship between Mexico and the United States, which is particularly marked at this border since any decision on either side of the wall can be seen reflected on the other side. It's like a disfigured echo that changes the receiver's perception, and automatically reconfigures and labels the emitter.

In *Culturas híbridas, estrategias para entrar y salir de la modernidad*, Néstor García Canclini (1989) sees this Tijuana, and sees the Tijuana–San Diego border next to cities like New York as a laboratory of postmodernity linking both countries and their inhabitants in constant commercial trade—legal and illegal, I would add. Regarding Tijuana, Garcia Canclini observes that the multicultural character of the city is expressed in the use of Spanish, English, and other indigenous languages spoken in the neighborhoods and the *maquiladoras*, and between those selling handicrafts downtown.

Nevertheless, this hybridization to which Garcia Canclini refers causes a controversy between the insiders and the outsiders of Tijuana ethnography, so that for city specialists like Heriberto Yépez: "I think postmodernism ruined a lot of things. One of them was the understanding of Tijuana. Tijuana is a lot of more than hybridism. Tijuana is all about tensions. Disencounters. A city of farewell to Hegel. A city beyond synthesis" (Montezemolo, 2006: 80).

Recently, the academic and essayist himself has again quoted this concept writing that the hybridism is being replaced by another model, a kind of border rudology: a discourse no longer focused on the exaltation and cataloging of crosses or mixtures of imaginaries, materialities, and identities but in the administration of ruins or residuals of others (Yépez, 2018: 975). It is these conceptual transformations that have fascinated many scholars who study the border.

Thus, Tijuana seeks the illusion of taking on the world because apparently there is very little left to tell about the city on the other side, San Diego, California. As of July 2018, San Diego had a population of 3,343,364, of which 34% were Latinos or Hispanics (CENSUS Bureau, 2019). It is in the State of California, which is one of the most economically and politically important states in the United States, not to mention having the largest concentration of the county's Navy activities there. California is the fifth largest economy in the world. If we think of California as its own country, it would economically surpass countries like the United Kingdom and France (Ejel, 2018). To the north of San Diego is Los Angeles, to the west is the Pacific Ocean, to the east is El Centro, and to the south is Tijuana, Mexico.

San Diego has been the headquarters of military bases since the Spanish-American War of 1898. Thus, we understand that its main economic activity revolved around the installation of its military bases, which boosted the real estate and commercial activity of the city. As Abe Shragg points out:

> San Diegans always saw this position, geographical position, as one that was of primary importance, not only for the defense of the west coast but as the United States became increasingly interested in Pacific Rim affairs, especially after the Spanish American War of 1898, this seemed to San Diegans a logical place for that. Business people in San Diego also saw a great opportunity to harness the resources of the federal government to develop the bay and to increase opportunities for urban expansion. And by the turn of the 20th century, that became a primary goal of the San Diego Chamber of Commerce to make the city grow.
>
> (Finn, 2009)

From the soldiers stationed in San Diego, the relationship with and the myth of the city of Tijuana began. San Diego became a city of transit that

Hollywood celebrities had to pass through in order to reach the Tijuana paradise, especially during Prohibition. As Steven Brender wrote in his book *Run for the Border: Vice and Virtue in U.S.-Mexico Border Crossings*:

Tijuana benefited from its proximity to populous Southern California and to Hollywood when the advent of the talking motion pictures coincided with the Prohibition era. During the dry years, Tijuana became Hollywood's playground, with stars flying in from Los Angeles aboard Ford trimotor airplanes. . . . Tijuana's crown jewel of chic decadence, the Casino Agua Caliente opened in 1928 and was a magnet for celebrities.

(Brender, 2012: 58)

If indeed California's upper class benefited from a paradise of alcohol and gaming, different ranks of the military class were also attracted by their southern neighbor. This created the first economic link between the two cities, a sometimes-silent complicity, that continues to this day.

The city of San Diego has also been nurtured by various migrations, not only the Latinos or Spanish speakers who cross the border daily to work legally or illegally there. A number of Asian, Middle Eastern, and African migrants also permeate the streets of downtown. On an afternoon in downtown San Diego, one can pick out a range of sounds mixed with the industrial sounds of construction and cars. According to information provided by the University of Southern California (USC), in 2012 there were 698,000 migrants living in San Diego, which represented 23% of the total population. From 2008 to 2010, the origin of these migrants was: 47% from Mexico, 13% from the Philippines, 5% from China, Vietnam, and Iraq, and 30% from other countries (Pastor *et al.*, 2012: 29). In his article "By the Numbers: How Diverse is Your Neighborhood?" published in 2014, Leonardo Castañeda tells us:

When Tau Baraka was growing up, southeastern San Diego was already a pretty diverse community. Baraka, now 47 and the owner of Imperial Barbershop in Encanto, said that back then the area was primarily white, African-American and Hispanic.
"But as the years start progressing, you start seeing a big change in that, especially with the Filipino population here" Baraka said. . . . Now, neighborhoods in southeastern San Diego, including Encanto, Paradise Hills and Skyline, are home to sizable Filipino, Samoan, and West and East African populations. . . . If the eastern part of San Diego is the most diverse, the coast is the most homogenous. And in this case, homogenous does mean mostly white. Point Loma, Ocean Beach and La Jolla are among the least diverse neighborhoods in the city. Ocean Beach,

for example, is 80 percent white and has a diversity index of .24. That makes it the fifth least diverse community in San Diego.

(Castañeda, 2014)

In 2018, Castañeda wrote a similar article titled "By the Numbers: San Diego County's Most Diverse Neighborhoods":

> When two residents in the southeastern San Diego neighborhood of Encanto meet, there's a 71 percent chance they're of different racial and ethnic backgrounds. In the coastal community of Cardiff, there's only a 25 percent chance of that happening. Local non-profits and elected leaders often praise multicultural and inclusive communities, but measuring real diversity is not often as clear cut. . . . That makes Encanto one of the most diverse neighborhoods in San Diego County, and Cardiff one of the least diverse. That doesn't surprise Brian Pollard, chief executive of The Urban Collaborative Project, a non-profit focused in part on health and safety issues in southeastern San Diego. He also sees the diversity as a positive. "The diversity that I experience is a very healthy one", Pollard said. "You can see the art that's appearing all over Southeast San Diego now. It depicts the cultures; it depicts a lot of history and a lot of looking forward".

(Castañeda, 2018)

Those cultural diversities are what has made San Diego not just a cosmopolitan city, but above all multicultural. However, as shown in Castañeda's texts, San Diego is well divided in zones by the economic level of its inhabitants, which also defines the cultural group that lives there and thus its sounds. San Diego has historically been a city where you can find opposites: a society in one part very conservative, and in another part, open and diverse. To some extent, it is a military economy that is also open to international trade. It is a city that has one of the most important zoos in the world, a major league baseball team, a racetrack, one of the highest-ranking universities in the world, several symphony orchestras, and an opera company. And, it is the city with the fourth-largest homeless population in the United States (Wart, 2018).

On the City of San Diego's official website, Mayor Kevin L. Faulconer speaks about the city:

> From our spectacular coast to scenic communities to scientific innovations, new opportunities start in San Diego every day. The City of San Diego is committed to serving all our neighborhoods, fostering an

economically prosperous community and creating a world-class city for
all. Together, we're building our better future.

(Faulconer, n.d.)

For many years, this is what San Diego officially looked like, with the
motto "America's finest city". In 2007, *San Diego Magazine* launched a contest for the city's motto. Among the many proposals, I am struck by some
such as:

"San Diego: City of Class", "Gateway to Tijuana", "The City of Diver-
sity", "Tijuana's Big Sister", "San Diego, the Perfect Place to Die", "The
City of Elegance", "San Diego: A City Like a Fine Wine", "San Diego!
Mexican Port of Entry to Los Angeles", "San Diego: Summer City".

(San Diego Magazine, 2007)

These contrasting realities are what make the Tijuana–San Diego border
so special since the mixture of cultures functionally complement each other
both internally and externally.

In a conversation published in the book *Aquí es Tijuana*, sociologist and
activist Mike Davis describes how he saw these two cities years ago:

I grew up along the border in the 1950s and early 1960s. The two most
important events in my adolescence were joining the civil rights movement (Congress of Racial Equality) in San Diego when I was sixteen
(1962) and—innately related—discovering a new world across the border. San Diego in this period was a segregated, reactionary city with a
stifling civic culture, dominated by the San Diego Union, and zero toler-
ance for leftish or unorthodox ideas. Rebellious, incipiently radical kids
like me hung out at a few "beatnik" coffee houses or in the basement of
Wahrenbrooks' Bookstore downtown. But we only really felt free when
we had crossed the border. Tijuana was our portal to an entire universe
of forbidden and wonderful ideas. My first exposure, for example, to
the immerse heritage of European Marxism and Critical Theory was
at the old El Día bookstore off Revolution. In Tijuana we met Spanish
Republicans, listened to lore from elderly Villistas, and debated politics
with sophisticated college students. It was in Tijuana that I first began to
appreciate the impact of the Cuban Revolution and was first able to see
the U.S. civil rights struggle in larger perspective. Tijuana also kindled
the desire to keep going southward, toward that great other America we
learned nothing about in schools. Most San Diego high school kids in
this era, of course, crossed the border to drink, insult locals, and leave

behind a trail of vomit and bad manners. We hated that. Tijuana for us was a little bit of Paris, our personal Left Bank, and my fondness for the city and the cultural freedom it represented has never waned.

(Montezemolo *et al.*, 2006: 31)

Both borders have collaborated in their mutual economic and cultural growth. Talking about one of them is talking about the other, like defining yourself by seeing your reflection. Much of it is defined by its surroundings, and although the sounds manage to intermingle, they also separate and define.

The Sound Border

The voices didn't join in this time, as she hadn't spoken, but to her great surprise, they all thought in chorus (I hope you understand what thinking in chorus means-for I must confess that I don't), "Better say nothing at all. Language is worth a thousand pounds a word".

Through the Looking Glass
(Carrol, 1896: 40)

Identifying the sounds characteristic of Tijuana and San Diego is a kind of enchantment. When one arrives at the border, everything seems louder and more visual. Forgotten sounds from the past resurface trying "to make you listen" and give signals about the city that contains them. Maybe they are more audible due to the contrasts of the two borders, or due to the same disparities at the national and international level. In a conversation with Heriberto Yépez, he told me: "the myth of Tijuana is there, let yourself be carried away by that Tijuana and that border" (Yépez, 2019). Part of the search for these sounds is based on that spell of the contrasts that arise and happen naturally.

On a walk through both cities, we encounter sounds that do not correspond with what should commonly be heard in a city. Consequently, we begin to discard features of the soundscape. Robert Murray Schafer mentions that in a soundscape we can identify certain features. He calls them *keynote sounds*, *signal sounds*, and *sound marks*, and also *archetypal sounds*. He defines *keynote sounds* as all sounds heard by chance, unconsciously perhaps as listening to them happens unnoticed. However, they become common sounds constantly heard. *Signal sounds* refer to the sounds that we are conscious of in some way, becoming a signal or figure that gives us the opportunity to interpret them. *Soundmark* refers to a distinct place where the sound is characteristic. Finally, *archetypal sounds* are those sounds that we have inherited and that are extremely symbolic (Murray, 1994: 9–10).

Even though these details do help in creating a categorization of sound types, in the case of this study, said categorization would only compartmentalize sounds arbitrarily, and not delve into the sounds emanating from both cities. I think this has been the main error in some of the soundscape studies, staying in this simple classification without contextualizing the problem socially. Other techniques must be included to identify the sounds of a place by mapping where they are happening, achieving a "dimensional sonology", as I like to call it. The case of the Tijuana–San Diego border is revealing as a case study because we can appreciate the challenge of identifying or at least placing the sounds produced by one city and immersed in the other, and sounds that stay anchored in one city regardless of socio-geographical circumstances.

In this context, our work settles into the search for those dimensional sonologies, not from the archetypes or the collective imagination but from discovering the characteristics of the society and the space it inhabits based on the sounds of daily life. These same sounds give us the key to understanding the society that inhabits and creates multiple sound spaces.

To achieve a dimensional sonology, it is necessary to listen to the sound identity from an individual, collective, and multidimensional position. By individual listening, I am referring to each person's perception of the sounds around them from which they form their own system of codes and understanding that may or may not coincide with the collective listening that is composed of the results of diverse listeners.

Finally, we observe multidimensional listening which I will base on this careful hearing that is achieved from seeing the different dimensions and movements that have a sound in different areas: geographic, social, and economic. We will have to look at the relationships that they generate in these areas by comparing and confronting them and their social realities. An example of this is the sound of the means of transportation that are generated in both border cities. Analyzing those sounds in particular leads us to identify diverse economic and social conditions of the users and, at the same time, a temporary transport to different eras thus coming to a sound idea in dynamic perspective of what is the society that it inhabits.

We also need to consider that sounds travel, change, and transform in each place and moment. But when we take a sample, we get signs or clues from those who produce them, a sort of x-ray of the city. It means going into what is there even though we don't see it, and recognizing that, yes it has always existed and accompanied us. Murray Shafer says that the ear is the only sense that doesn't close. I will add that it is the only one that is both in our consciousness and unconsciousness. That is why we can attribute meaning and connections to things, and in the specific case of sounds, what no other sense can give.

To reach this, it is necessary to have a type of "deep listening". Walking the streets of Tijuana or San Diego can be joyful if one's ears are wide open.

We can locate contrasting and over-the-top soundscapes; a multidimensionality is thrown into our listening. The American composer and accordionist Pauline Oliveros created the concept as well as the technique and practice of listening called *Deep Listening*, which she defined as follows: "This question is answered in the process of practicing listening with the understanding that the complex wave forms continuously transmitted to the auditory cortex from the outside world by the ear require active engagement with attention" (Oliveros, 2005: xxi).

Oliveros clearly distinguishes the difference between listening and hearing: "To hear and to listen have a symbiotic relationship with somewhat interchangeable common usage. I differentiate to hear and to listen. To hear is the physical means that enables perception. To listen is to give attention to what is perceived both acoustically and psychologically" (Oliveros, 2005: xxiii). This technique immerses us in the perception of sounds in a more complex way. It requires us to find the details of a sound within a specific space and time. That space-time dimension to which they belong immediately prompts us to reflect on the relationship of the sound and its meaning, rather the meaning that we cause. Likewise, it creates an immediate awareness of our environment and our place in it.

With respect to the relationship between sound and place, Steven Feld in his writing "Waterfall of song" explains the term coined as acoustemology, saying:

> Acoustemology means an exploration of Sonic sensibilities, specifically of ways in which sound is central to making sense, to knowing, to experiential truth. This seems particularly relevant to understanding the interplay of sound and felt balance in the sense and sensuality of emplacement, of making place. For places are as potentially reverberant as they are reflective, and one's embodied experiences and memories of them may draw significantly on the interplay of that resoundingness and reflectiveness.
>
> (Feld, 2018: 97)

It is this consciousness of place that makes sound take on meaning apart from the multidimensional consciousness of listening.

So, the sound begins to acquire meaning within an acoustic territory that can help us to understand ourselves. In his book *Acoustic Territories/Sound Culture and Everyday Life*, Brandon LaBelle writes:

> the presentation of specific acoustic territories should not be exclusively read as places or sites but more as itineraries, as point of departure as well as arrival. As territories, I define them as movements between and

among differing forces, full of multiplicity. Exposing them to listening I also map them onto an auditory paradigm, exploring them through a particular discourse, while allowing them to deepen my own listening, to influence and infect what I have so far imagined sound providing— intimacy, in provocative and complex scale. Sound creates a relational geography that is most often emotional, contentious, fluid, and which stimulates a form of knowledge that moves in and out the body.

Detailing the micro-epistemologies and everyday terrains of auditory experience, I've come to hear sound as a movement that gives us each other, as both gift and threat, as generosity and agitation, as laughter and tears, making listening as a highly provocative and relational sense.

(Labelle, 2010: XXV)

I have collected the examples of these border sonologies through a series of recordings made during personal sound walks, sometimes random and sometimes predetermined, which have been placed on a website for open consultation.[4] I have also referenced the recordings taken from the SONVI[5] platform, a project developed at the Autonomous University of Baja California (UABC) that captures the sounds to create a sound memory but also as a way to classify the sounds captured. There, part of the captured sounds were placed in a database used to perform the analysis of three sound categories.[6]

Sonologies of the Tijuana–San Diego Border

The snoring got more distinct every moment, and sounded more like a tune . . .
Through the Looking Glass
(Carroll, 1896: 134)

The border is a sound city often without purposeful or inadvertent noticing. Remaining in my childhood reminiscences of the border is a sound made by the pedestrians when crossing it upon returning to Mexico at San Ysidro-Tijuana, also known as the Puerta Mexico. Every time someone crossed the border, they had to pass through a metal revolving gate that caused a loud noise. With the creation of a new border entrance in 2012 called El Chaparral, that sound was no longer heard. That characteristic sound at the border (which I imagine said "you are in a new country, welcome to Mexican sonority") disappeared with the original crossing, thus part of its sound history was lost. However, in my last sound tours while recording in downtown Tijuana, I again heard that sound. The revolving metal gate had been installed in a square built in 2016 on the site of former police barracks. Seeking information about it, only photographs of the square's opening were found including excellent images of the sound sculpture. There was no information nor mention of the gate. It only mentioned that there is a sculpture project by the students of the Faculty of Arts at UABC (Uniradio, 2016). Arguably, homage was unintentionally paid to this Tijuana sound. This perhaps insignificant or unnoticed detail shows us the sound produced when turning the gate was the first link to a city and a benchmark of sound type.

This relocated door (Figure 1.2) creates a new soundscape with a very intense meaning for past generations because it transports us to a Tijuana at

Figure 1.2 Metal Revolving Gate, Now Relocated to Plaza de la Ocho, Tijuana

the turn of the century or even the middle of the last century. It represents a temporal and territorial displacement with its constant elemental metallic sound—a squeak after several turns and the repeated metallic percussion. So, what happens when a sound is heard that belongs to a specific time and space? The sound manages to immediately move one to another space-time dimension and acquires the meaning of the memory and at the same time the border membership. A kind of sensory quantum result manages to place us in various dimensions.

One of the first academic texts that I found in my search for the border sounds was *Playing the Fence, Listening to the Line: Sound, Sound Art, and Acoustic Politics at the US-Mexico Border* (Kun, 2011) by Josh Kun, who mentions a person who more than 20 years ago managed to realize the richness and sound transposition that exists at this border.

Octavio Hernández made several sound recordings of Tijuana and San Diego between 2016 and 2017 for the project *Sonic Zoo: Noise, Sound, and Rhythm on the Border Between Two Worlds*. This sound project was sponsored by inSite.[7] Hernández, along with a team of students from the bachelor of communications program at UABC, the so-called Sound Hunter Squadron,[8] launched themselves, recorders in hand, to capture the essence of Tijuana's sounds. Several of these original recordings on 90-minute cassettes can be found in the Archivo Histórico de Tijuana in the Colección Octavio Hernández. Here also can be found a cassette labelled "Insite 97 / Zoo/Pre mix", which contains recordings of interviews of people in Tijuana and San Diego, a boxing match, a street musician playing a bolero on public transportation, and the sound of the San Diego trolley, among other sounds characteristic of both cities. This cassette, from the project of soundscape recordings, culminated in a mix made by Pepe Mogt, founder and member of Nortec. Sound contrasts are made by inserting rhythmic atmospheres and processing the recordings. The disk has 13 audio tracks and was presented at inSITE97.[9]

In the accompanying compact disk booklet, Hernández describes the project:

> This record is dedicated to the streets and its inhabitants, mythic characters in the Sonic symphony of everyday. And to the memory of Humberto Lavin, midnight sax player extraordinaire.
>
> On both sides of the border, noise is the music of the streets, of things and matter in motion. It is the language of human activity, the eternal hymn "I make noise, therefore I exist". It is code that transcends languages, nationalities, classes, races and creeds. It is something you grow used to, that loses its magic out routine. We are noise and we move around in this pandemonium.

(Hernández, 1997)

These 13 recordings can be heard at UCSD[10] in the digital collection. It is a sound record of a time, mixed with a techno bit, that tries to put us in that present, a faraway present for us as far away as the field recordings of the stories from the two borders compiled by Hernández and his team. The set of all these recordings is a kind of sound novel, a passing of any citizen who crosses the border from the south to the north or from the north to the south. It's as if Hernández told stories of the inhabitants of a sound zoo at the border of two worlds.

The first example with which I begin the study of sonological dimensions is a personal anecdote. While reviewing Hernández's materials in the Archivo Histórico de Tijuana, there were three students from the bachelor of history program of UABC who were doing some research. When I asked where to find a record shop and how to get there, we began to talk. I guess the generation gap caused them to be curious. I hope they didn't see me as part of the historical archives. I began to tell them about this border soundscape project and its contrasts. One of them immediately said: "It's true. We don't have the trolley sound; we only have the old *calafias*".[11]

This sound reference led me to reflect on the character of public transportation on each side of the border for decades and how both are transformed in the same way as their sounds when crossing the border. So, I decided to take a trip across the border from downtown Tijuana to downtown San Diego to hear the sonorities.

Just as many citizens use public transportation daily to cross the border, I felt a bit like the pilgrim in *The Divine Comedy* although without the help of Virgilio. I set out to start my voyage from downtown Tijuana at eight o'clock in the morning in front of the Church of Guadalupe, an old Tijuana cathedral. I could hear an intense movement of people walking hurriedly in many directions, merchants sweeping their sidewalks, the local radio, all intermingled with the sound of cars. After a few minutes, I managed to find the transportation that would take me to the "line": an old blue and white bus announced the trip with its squeal of brakes and motor. When the bus stopped, the second sound I heard was the squeak of the doors opening. And there precisely began the delicacy of sounds as the bus headed to its destination.

Besides the sound of the brakes, I heard the metallic sound of the body that made a loud rumble at each pothole we hit on the road. The occupied seats could be heard moving, as apparently they were not well screwed down. Continuing to concentrate on the sounds of the bus for the approximately ten-minute trip, I heard the motor, whose sound sharpened with each gear shift or when stopped at a crossing. The penetrating sound of a maladjusted motor was highlighted, and during the whole trip, I heard as incidental music the melody and lyrics of a Sinaloan band's narcocorrido. Our trip ended with the shout "Line", which was the signal that we had to get off. In front of me was an elderly man with a cane that hit the floor hard as he went down the stairs of the bus. He thanked the driver, whose response was silence.

The sound of the bus was heard seconds later after the passengers had gotten off as if the motor was saying goodbye. There was a sound interlude while crossing a large bridge from which you could see the cars below waiting in line to cross the border. There weren't many—about 150 per lane with 20 lanes open. Crossing the bridge, you could hear cars passing quickly on one side, a machine drilling the pavement, and more lightly, some food and handicraft merchants offering their merchandise to the people in their cars in line waiting to cross to the United States. Already close to the border in the pedestrian line to cross, several horns, an airplane passing overhead, and some voices of those who distribute merchandise to the sellers could be heard. Other voices, those of the people who were about to cross the border, intermingled in English and Spanish. For an instant, I heard another language which I deduced was French. With the shout of a migration employee, I knew that I must go to the side to get out of the way because a group of migrants, that I deduced were Haitians, were led to the pedestrian border gate by members of the Instituto Nacional de Migración. Near the gate, a woman was singing for some coins, in return giving a stick of gum. Also, the shrill sound of a bus that takes people from the border to Northern California was heard. Crossing the border, silence suddenly broke in. I turned off the recorder for the security measures of the United States.

After inspection by the American agents, conversation in Spanish was again heard, with the noise of luggage wheels accompanying the voices. Another airplane was heard passing overhead along with the sound of the helicopters that fly over the border area. A sharp sound arose from an imposing Tranvia or Red Trolley, and nearby the sound of a bus motor was heard. Both are part of public transportation system. In the distance, a bell signaled to motorists that a trolley would soon cross the road. I pressed the button to open the trolley door, got on, and began my trip to downtown San Diego.

Suddenly, as the trolley prepared to depart, there was a futuristic type sound. When the doors closed, the sound was deep and serious. The trip began with route and security messages heard in English and in Spanish. They told us that we were on the blue line. For all 17 stations prior to arriving in downtown San Diego, the passengers were told the name of the next station prior to arriving and what it was upon arrival. The trip was relatively silent except for the air conditioning, the doors opening, and the safety bell that sounded when the doors were closing. When we arrived at the second last station, an African American got on the train with a tape recorder and began to listen to some Christian pop. Seconds later, an older Asian couple spoke in a mixture of English and an Asian language. They were lost as they had missed their station. The silence accompanied by the pop music was interrupted by a request for help from these Asians. When getting off the trolley at Santa Fe Station, the only sound heard was the trolley. It seemed as if the city was a desert as I walked a few meters toward one of the main streets. In general, the soundscape of the city was silence.

The sonological dimension that I heard here is distinct, as if the looking glass in Alice's living room had been crossed and everything that was on the other side was turned upside down. If we compare the sounds of transportation in Tijuana with those of San Diego, in many senses we see opposites that are much more than cultural factors. Table 1.1 shows some of the characteristic sounds of this trip.

While the amount of sounds may be similar, the type of sound of each form of transportation is completely distinct. Without the intention of passing a value judgment, we can appreciate that the sounds produced by the Mexican bus have to do with its structure, that is, the incomplete worn structure. The sound level is much more complex. On the American trolley, the majority of the sounds are to create safety and comfort for the passengers. Except for the sound created between two people, there was no interaction between the users and the trolley itself. It seems that we are facing a mirror-like sonological dimension, sonorities that give us clues as to the daily behavior of a society.

Another special case of contrasts and temporary space displacements occurs in cities, in particular in the downtown areas. In the heart of the cities lives part of the soul of that city. A kind of synthesis and its reflection are in the sounds that are captured in the small streets which are full of meanings, evocations, and memories. As Italo Calvino observes,

> cities are a set of many things: memories, wishes and signs of a language. They are places of barter as explained in all the history books about the economy. But this bartering is not just about merchandise; it is also bartering words, wishes, memories.
>
> (Calvino, 1997: 15)

Table 1.1 Transportation Sounds

Tijuana (Bus)	San Diego (Trolley)
Brake pads	Engine
Metallic body sounds	Air conditioning
Motor speed changes	Bilingual station announcements
Music of *corridos*	Security door
Motors	Conversation of Asians
Shouts of the driver announcing the stops	A passenger's music
Moving bus chairs	
The gear shift	

In the same way, listening to the downtown areas of Tijuana and San Diego give us a clue about their daily and everyday dynamics. A sound dimension and a linguistic dimension are sometimes confused. At moments, we can doubt which side of the border we are on. Hearing downtown Tijuana sounds leads us to discover a series of sounds of the society itself. For example, on Calle Segunda y Avenida Constitución, there is the possibility of hearing an Aztecan dancer who arrived from San Cristobal de las Casas, Chiapas (Figure 1.3). At the same time, you can hear rap, *norteña*, rock, and endless styles

Figure 1.3 Aztecan Dancer and *Norteño* Musician, Tijuana

of music that come from cars. Sometimes, these same public buses break into this music with a symphony of horns.

Crossing the street, I found a "Pajarito de la suerte", a tradition of telling a customer's future. The shouts of the crier encouraged the bird to greet and draw several small cards, which were then read in a loud voice with a special intonation. Minutes later, two people of the Christian faith arrived at the same corner with tape recorders and Christian music that added to the sonorities. A few meters on Avenida Constitución between Segunda and Tercera was the *calafia* stop with their respective spokesmen who shouted the exit and direction of the bus: "come on, come on, going to the border, going to the border, there's still space" in a nasal tone. This was repeated, sometimes changing the direction to which it is directed. Sometimes the crosswalk warning sound was heard, accompanied by the music of the street vendors. When I stayed at this same crossing, I suddenly saw the pedestrian street Santiago Argüello, which took me to Plaza Santa Cecilia where I heard groups of mariachis waiting for customers. The sound surprise on that street was that not only did I hear mariachis offering their songs to tourists but also a *norteña* band from Sinaloa, a romantic trio, and a group of girls singing with speakers in the center of the plaza. There was a massive sound polyphony on a single street, including the rock music in English coming from the restaurants.

Another example of multidimensionality comes from a mixture of sounds from diverse cultures and regions in a common time and space disassociated in another parallel time and space. The dimensional sonology that I heard here doesn't end. I continued on Calle Revolución, where I encountered sellers of pharmaceuticals, souvenirs or "curios" as they say in Tijuana, the hailers for the restaurants and bars, and the Burritos-Cebras photographers (Figure 1.4) speaking a very special English, Anglo-Saxon phonetics with a Tijuanense pronunciation. This sound displacement of languages, like the defense sounds, shows what Tijuana is and the constant listening of the English language they manage to mix. A sound ecosystem is conjugated, perhaps unique to the Mexican border.

If we compare this to downtown San Diego, there are many contrasts. Although it is true that being on the immediate side of the US border causes linguistic confusion when you hear people speaking Spanish, including the migration police and people in businesses, shops, and shopping centers, they are dominated by the sounds of Spanish whose sound is less strident with a lower volume. Little by little the volume of the sounds diminishes as one crosses the border. At the point of crossing the border, a great silence accompanies the wait for the migration officers to ask for your papers to then let you cross or send you to secondary inspection, a place that is even more silent.

Heading to downtown San Diego, a fading of sound happens in the intensity as well as the number of sounds that are heard. There are some

Figure 1.4 Burrito-Cebra, Tijuana

sound spots of languages other than the native language, although they are minimal. My journey to downtown San Diego happened around 10:30 a.m. When I got off the trolley at the Santa Fe station, I began a sound journey on Broadway Avenue accompanied by the sound of some cars. The first sound I recognized was at the bus stop when I heard the sound of the motor as the bus arrived. The sound of the safety alarm when opening and closing the doors was striking.

Following my path, I observed some people on the sidewalk talking quietly. There were very few people talking, maybe one or two per block. Two hundred meters after resuming my journey, construction sounds broke the silence of the streets. Some sounds of the pedestrian crossing emitted by traffic signals coincided with my route. The sound of a fire truck and passing cars accompanied me for several minutes until a person approached me and asked what I was doing. He demanded that I ask for permission to take photographs and record the city, arguing that it was an invasion of his privacy. No doubt he was a civilian worried about his safety. After explaining that the purpose of my recordings was for an academic project and that I belonged to a university, he stopped his demands and let me continue with my work. He got on a bus, and I continued my walk.

It surprised me that I didn't encounter any contrasting sonorities on the streets, just the regular sound of cars except for some interrupting sounds of skateboards, an ambulance, and a couple of birds flying overhead. At three minutes to eleven in the morning, I stopped for a few minutes at the Broadway and Third Street crossing where I managed to capture more sounds of cars, more birds, traffic signals, and talking. Continuing my walk, I arrived at a shopping center, where the sound of a water fountain mixed with music coming from some speakers and a man and his dog playing in another fountain. I went deeper into downtown San Diego. My next encounter was with a homeless person who approached me to ask why I was recording. He was much friendlier than the first character that had confronted me blocks earlier. He also asked me where he could hear the sounds and if it was part of public radio.

Some construction sounds mixed with the car sounds and, on one occasion, with an alarm. The sonorities were generally homogenous with only two incidents interrupting the peacefulness. The first was a homeless person fearlessly riding a bicycle at full speed, shouting loudly at the pedestrians to warn them. The second incident was a couple of, I believe, Koreans who were arguing loudly in the middle of the sidewalk along with some physical violence. After a tour of about two hours in the downtown area, I decided to stop the day's recording.

Once again, Table 1.2 shows the variety of sounds found in the downtown areas of both cities.

The quantity of sounds that were heard in the downtown area of the cities announce a disparity as two sound dimensions were found in these cities. In Tijuana, the number of sounds as well as their volume intermingle, while in San Diego, except for the sound of cars that is usually constant, there were less sounds that were sporadic and at a lower decibel. There was a disproportion in the amount of sounds and in the way they were produced. A contrasting characteristic was that in Mexico all the sounds intermingle, while in the United

Table 1.2 Sounds of the City

Tijuana	San Diego
Cars	Cars
People speaking	People speaking
Traffic lights	Traffic lights
Music: *norteña*, mariachi, etc.	Music in the shopping center
Aztecan dancer	Construction
Street sellers	Fountain
Fortune teller and card reader	Birds
Radio or TV from the restaurants	Homeless people
Christians professing their faith	
Bus spokespersons	
Car horns	
Music in the cars	
Burritos-Cebra photographers	

States it appeared that each one waited its turn to appear and disappear. This reminds me of a phrase from Cortázar about the city in which he says that the city is like that. One enters and leaves there without asking permission and without being asked. And that he thinks it was always like that (Cortázar, 1995: 43).

For my third example of these dimensional sonologies, I once again want to make an intense sound contrast, that of the west border. The first sound shock that was heard (and that was the detonator of this project) was found in Tijuana Beach and San Diego Beach. These beaches are divided by a big fence that extends into the ocean and, on either side, any sound or image recorded will be shocking. It makes you feel like a great field recorder or a great photographer of customs or a naturalist. I will start by describing the sonority of San Diego's beach, where this sound journey begins.

To arrive at the border wall that divides the ocean, one would need to walk on one of two paths about two kilometers to Border Field State Park, a natural reserve. On either path, what is constant are the sounds of the birds that inhabit the reserve. The predominant sounds along the way are those of a helicopter that flies security routes close to the border, and on some occasions, several helicopters practicing because of the proximity to the Naval Outlying Landing of Imperial Beach. The sound of the helicopters is a constant that on occasion does not allow you to recognize the nature sounds of that reserve.

Arriving at the beach, one can see a small space that is known as Friendship Park where in the past, you could talk freely or even kiss between the bars that separated the two countries. Families from both countries would meet there. On some occasions, the door that is there would be opened for a few minutes so that migrants could hug their family members from the other side of the border, and then each would return to their side. According to Kate Morrisey (2018), these rules have been changed since 2018 so that now the sounds of families gathered from both sides is infrequent.

To be at the American beach, the dominant sounds were the waves breaking and then diluting in the sand, seagulls and other marine birds that fly overhead, on some occasions the wind, the passage of a visitor who wished to contemplate the sunset in silence, and rarely the radio of the Border Patrol reporting an incident. Like a faraway, diluted sound, one wished hear the murmurs of people and some mixed sounds that came from the other side of the metal wall. Those sounds, a kind of sound shadow, were echoes of the other sound dimension, a contrast. At times it was hard to believe that after walking for more than an hours, all that had been heard were natural sounds except for the helicopter. Listening again to the active sounds of society could be shocking.

But what were those sounds that originate from the same beach divided by the great metal wall that cuts into the ocean? They were sounds of a society that did not seem to notice how much happened loudly. They were just having fun on the Mexican side when they entered what is known as el Parque de la Amistad (Friendship Park). You heard the proclamation of a man dressed in white shouting "massages!" accompanied by the sound of a sharp little bell announcing the *paletero*. The music of a *norteña* group coming from a restaurant near the beach arrived forcefully thanks to the wind. Curiously, the only sound that united the two borders was the sound of the ocean, also divided by the metal wall. As I approached the beach, the sounds intermingled even more. Children playing and yelling could be heard along with the music from their parents' tape recorders. One after another street musicians offered their services. But the sound that continued all the time was the sharp and penetrating sounds of the *paletero*'s bells. Now there was not just one but various bells coming from different places, a kind of envelope of bell sounds. While walking along the beach, there were the voices of children and adults. All kinds of talking could be found, sometimes in different languages.

Leaving the beach and heading again to Friendship Park, there was a religious group giving a Sunday service. Once again, the sounds intermingled, creating a strange result. The combination was a bilingual religious service accompanied by a singer and a guitar, the shout of "massages!", a person lying on the ground maybe trying to sleep—perhaps due to the effects of drugs or alcohol—*norteña* music from the restaurant, voices of curious tourists, and constantly the ocean and the bell of the *paletero* (Figure 1.5).

If we make a comparative table of the constant sounds on both beaches (Table 1.3), the result is revealing since the amount and type of sounds at each of the borders is significant.

The main sounds from the American side were of nature while the sounds from the Mexican beach were human and societal sounds. Two mirror-shaped dimensions were shown again.

Figure 1.5 Paletero, Tijuana Beach

Table 1.3 Sounds of the Beach

Tijuana	San Diego
Norteña music	Birds
Children's screams	Wind
Massage crier	Air
Ocean	Ocean
People's voices	Helicopter
Paletero's bell	
Music from radios/recorders	
Religious service	
Tourists	
Street musicians	

Coming Out of the Looking Glass

Now Kitty, let's consider who it was that dreamed it all.
This is a serious question . . .
Which do you think it was?

Through the Looking Glass
(Carroll, 1896: 150)

Carrying out a study of the sonological dimensions of the border gives the observer a perspective as to how a society lives and its behavior. While sonology is a term that is used to describe any type of sound study, I have applied it to the study of the sounds of the border, looking at the multidimensionality that it offers. The sounds generate an infinite amount of information that provide a sociological perspective to its environment. Researcher Frances Dyson writes:

> Sound, as I have argued, offers a way to negotiate the "unthought" and the unspoken, to develop other vocabularies and other forms of political, economic, and social organization. Sound's ephemeral and atmospheric nature is, like the environment, something that circulates outside of exchange, and refocuses attention on the space and environment of the subject rather than the subject *per se*.
>
> (Dyson, 2014: 149)

Through its various dimensions, sound helps us to find and recognize ourselves, and in turn to transform or transport ourselves to other times and spaces. In this brief study of the border sonorities, we can find diverse sound dimensions where the sonorities emerge from the characteristics of its people and environment. A symbolic object like the revolving gate at the border crossing transforms our dimensional perception of time and space. A means of transportation that takes us to the same place can be different depending on the side of the border on which it is used. Each one has its own sounds that identify the place where we are; it helps us strengthen spatiality. "Listening" to the cities could be a reflection of the economic activity and customs of their people. The sounds rise and fall depending on where they are heard. Finally, through the study of sound, it becomes evident that a fence clearly makes two sound realities while managing to divide them at the same time; two sound dimensions of the same reality, a fact that invites us to continue looking at more sound characteristics in order to appreciate another dimension of society.

For now, we are left with those border sounds between Tijuana and San Diego which make it unique and enigmatic, as enigmatic as the end of the story *Through the Looking Glass*:

> Children yet, the tale to hear,
> Eager eye and willing ear,
> Lovingly shall nestle near.
>
> In a Wonderland they lie,
> Dreaming as the days go by,
> Dreaming as the summers die:
>
> Ever drifting down the stream—
> Lingering in the golden gleam—
> Life what is it but a dream?
>
> (Carroll, 1896: 151)

Notes

1. Term given to those who come from the same city or country in which they were born.
2. Small store with few resources and, therefore, poorly stocked; also any precarious establishment where a service is offered.
3. El Chaparral: port of entry between Tijuana–San Diego.
4. https://soundcloud.com/alvaro-diaz-944556578/sets/border-sounds-tijuana-san
5. www.proyectosonvi.com
6. It is worth mentioning that there is also a sound record of Tijuana in the Fonoteca of El Colegio de la Frontera Norte; however, it has only been used as a secondary reference, and the recordings found there have not been used directly in this study.
7. The project inSite is defined in its oficial page:

   Founded in 1992, inSite has completed five editions based in the San Diego/ Tijuana border region. It has had the good fortune to be able to commission some of the most significant artists from Mexico, the US, and elsewhere quite early in their careers. The main purpose of the program is to commission site-specific work by local and international artists following the curatorial guidelines of each edition.

8. This squadron was composed of Humberto Huerta, Liliana Willem, Ana Karina Mejía, Sandra Reyes, Rosalba Velásco, Luis Martínez, and Carlos V. González (Booklet CD Zoosonico).
9. On inSite's website, they explain a bit about that edition, saying that the project in Site'97 was an exhibition from September 26 to November 30, 1997, in the San Diego–Tijuana border region.
10. https://library.ucsd.edu/dc/object/bb50200841
11. If we speak about public transportation in Tijuana, we have to talk about "las calafias". They appeared for the first time in the year 1976. The word CALAFIA is the name of a legendary warrior with black skin. She ruled the island of California where only beautiful women lived. The story of Calafia was written in 1510 by García Rodríguez de Montalvo. Everything happens in the calafias and never stops. For Tijuanans, calafiero (the bus driver) is synonymous to brutish, vulgar, disheveled, with a bad taste in music, etc. But as everywhere, there are good and bad elements. Anything can happen on a calafia: a crash, a traffic jam, profanity, murders, robberies, and even a delivery. But what has not disappeared is the scandalous sound of their old motors and drivers, who day after day get up at 4 am to move thousands of Tijuanans to their destinations (Tijuana en el tiempo, 2017).

References

Albicker, S., Félix, C., París, D., Pérez Duperou, G., y Vélasco, L. (2017). *Emergencia migratoria y solidaridad de la sociedad civil en Tijuana, 2016–2017*. Tijuana: Colegio de la Frontera Norte.

Antiguo Cine Libertad. (2018, April 16). *Haiti Juana, Todo mundo se tiene que ir* [Video]. YouTube. www.youtube.com/watch?v=t2245rhw_gA

Archivo Histórico de Tijuana. *Colección Octavio Hernández*. Tijuana, Baja California, México.

Brender, S. (2012). *Run for the Border: Vice and Virtue in U.S.-Mexico Border Crossing*. New York: New York University Press.

Calvino, I. (1997). *Las Ciudades Invisibles*. Madrid: Ediciones Siruela.

Carroll, L. (1896). *Through the Looking Glass, and What Alice Found There*. The Project Gutenberg. Philadelphia: H. Altemus.

Castañeda, L. (2014, October 16). "By the Numbers: How Diverse Is Your Neighborhood?" *Inewsource*. https://inewsource.org/2014/10/16/diversity-in-san-diego/
————. (2018, January 15). "By the Numbers: San Diego County's Most Diverse Neighborhoods". *Inewsource*. https://inewsource.org/2018/01/15/san-diego-diverse-neigh borhoods/#methodology

Census Bureau. (2019). *QuickFacts: San Diego County, California, CA*. US Department of Commerce. www.census.gov/quickfacts/fact/table/sandiegocountycalifornia,CA/ PST045218

Colegio de la Frontera Norte, El. (2018, December 13). *La caravana de migrantes Centroamericanos en Tijuana 2018. Diagnóstico y propuesta de acción*. Tijuana: El Colegio de la Frontera Norte. www.colef.mx/wp-content/uploads/2018/12/EL-COLEF-Reporte-CaravanaMigrante-_-Actualizado.pdf

Cortázar, J. (1995). *62 / Modelo para armar*. Buenos Aires: Alfaguara.

Dyson, F. (2014). *The Tone of Our Times: Sound, Sense, Economy, and Ecology*. Cambridge, MA: Massachusetts Institute of Technology.

Ejel, B. (2018, May 4). "California Now World's Fifth-Largest Economy, Bigger Than Britain". *The Sacramento Bee*. www.sacbee.com/news/business/article210466514.html

Espacio Migrante. (2018, November 22). *Gran concierto Haiti-Juana 2* [Video]. Facebook. www.facebook.com/175756395879089/videos/1143093415845890/

Euronews. (2018, November 26). *Asalto masivo al muro de Tijuana* [Video]. You-Tube. www.youtube.com/watch?v=MWY4tc21H-0

Faulconer, K. (n.d.). "A Message from the Mayor". *The City of San Diego*. www.sandiego.gov/

Feld, S. (2018). "Waterfall of Song: An Acoustemology of Place Resounding in Bosavi, Papua New Guinea". In *Senses of Place*. Santa Fe, NM: School of American Research Press.

Finn, P. (Producer), & Cavannaugh, M. (Host). (2009, June 23). *The Military Is Embedded in San Diego's History* [Radio program]. San Diego, CA: KPBS. www.kpbs.org/news/2009/jun/23/military/

García Canclini. N. (1989). *Culturas híbridas. Estrategias para entrar y salir de la modernidad*. México: Grijalbo.

Hernández, O. (1997). *Zoo-Sónico: ruidos, sones y latidos en la frontera de dos mundos*. CD. [Liner notes]. Tijuana: Insite97.

Insite. *Insite*. http://insite.org.mx/wp/en/insite/

Instituto Nacional de Estadística y Geografía. (2015). *Cuéntame, Información por entidad*. Baja California. http://cuentame.inegi.org.mx/monografias/informacion/ bc/poblacion/default.aspx?tema=me&e=02

Instituto Nacional de Migración. (2019, July 19). *Permanecen 10 mil migrantes en BC*. INM. www.inm.gob.mx/gobmx/word/index.php/permanecen-10-mil-migrantes-en-bc/

Kun, J. (2011). "Playing the Fence, Listening to the Line: Sound, Sound Art, and Acoustic Politics at the US-Mexico Border". In Performance in the borderlands. New York: Palgrave Macmillan.

LaBelle, B. (2010). *Acoustic Territories/Sound Culture and Everyday Life*. New York: Continuum.

———. (2018). *Sonic Agency, Sound and Emergent Forms of Resistance*. London: Goldsmiths Press.

Montezemolo, F. (2006). "Tijuana, Became Rather That Being: representando representaciones. . . ". En *Culturas, agentes y representaciones sociales en Baja California*. Mexicali: Universidad Autónoma de Baja California/Miguel Ángel Porrua.

Montezemolo, F., Peralta, R., & Yépez, H. (2006). *Aquí es Tijuana!* London: Black Dog Publishing.

Morrisey, K. (2018, February 14). "Border Patrol Changes Rules at Friendship Park, Upsetting Frequent Visitors". *The San Diego Union-Tribune*. www.sandiegouniontribune.com/news/immigration/sd-me-friendship-park-20180214-story.html

Murray Schafer, R. (1994). *Our Sonic Environment and the Soundscape: The Tuning of the World*. Rochester: Destiny Books.

Oliveros, P. (2005). *Deep Listening: A Composer's Sound Practice*. Lincoln, NE: iUniverse.

Pastor, M., Ortiz, R., Carter, V., Scoggins, J., & Perez, A. (2012, September 12). *California Immigrant Integration Scorecard*. Los Ángeles: University of South California.

Pradilla, A. (2019). *Caravana: cómo el éxodo centroamericano salió de la clandestinidad*. México: Penguin Random House.

Ruzzi, S. (2014). "Al otro lado de Heriberto Yépez. Percepciones desde y sobre la frontera México-Estados Unidos". En *Act 29—Literaturas e culturas em Portugal e na América Hipânica. Novas perspectivas en diálogo*. V.N Farmalicão: Edições Humus.

San Diego Magazine. (2007, June 26). *San Diego Slogan Contest Entries*. www.sandiegomagazine.com/San-Diego-Magazine/November-1999/San-Diego-Slogan-Contest-Entries/index.php?cparticle=1&siarticle=0&requiressl=true#artanc

Sonic Zoo: Noise, Sound, and Rhythm on the Border Between Two Worlds. (1997). *InSite Archive. MSS 707*. Special Collections & Archives, UC San Diego. https://library.ucsd.edu/dc/object/bb50200841

Tijuana en el tiempo. (2017, December 27). *Las Calafias* [Facebook]. www.facebook.com/TijuanaenelTiempo/photos/a.38139021886450/560288277641309/?type=1&theater

TRACInmigration. (2018). *Judge-by-Judge Asylum Decisions in Immigration Courts: FY 2013–2018* (Graphic Highlights Immigration). Syracuse University. https://trac.syr.edu/immigration/reports/judge2018/denialrates.html

Uniradio Informa. (2016, April 9). "Este domingo inauguran plaza 'La Ocho'". *Uniradio. Informa*. www.uniradioinforma.com/noticias/tijuana/404527/este-domingo-inauguran-plaza-la-ocho.html

Warth, G. (2018, December 17). "San Diego Again has 4th-Largest Homeless Population in Nation". *The San Diego Union Tribune*. www.sandiegouniontribune.com/news/homelessness/sd-me-homeless-report-20181217-story.html

Yépez, H. (2006). *Tijuanologías*. Mexicali: Universidad Autónoma de Baja California.

———. (2018). "Nuevas Tijuanologías: del Hibridismo a las Rudologías en las estéticas fronterizas". *En Revista Iberoamericana*, 84(265). 975–993. https://doi.org/10.5195/reviberoamer.2018.7672

———. (2019). *Comunicación personal*. 12 de noviembre de 2019.

2 Network Platforms, Electronic Scenes, and Cultural Activism at the Tijuana–San Diego Border

The Performance of Border Critical Thinking in Young Artistic Movements in the Early 21st Century

Rossana Lara Velázquez

In order to halt illegal immigration, "Operation Gatekeeper" was implemented in1994 by the United States Border Patrol at the US–Mexico border near San Diego. Through this measure, the amount of fencing barriers as well as Border Patrol agents in the San Diego Sector—the busiest Border Patrol sector, located north of the cities of Tijuana and Tecate, Mexico—nearly doubled. It was in 1993, by the time of NAFTA's signing between Mexico, Canada, and the United States, that this sector "tallied 531,689 apprehensions out of a total of 1,263,490 Border Patrol apprehensions nationwide".[1] It was around those years that the 14-mile San Diego-Tijuana border fence—the so-called "Tortilla Wall"—was erected.

Contradictions between economic frontiers openness, establishment of a "free market" between both countries, and at the same time, the physical closure of the Tijuana–San Diego border to the United States, the precarization of labor through neoliberal policies, and criminalization of forced migrant labor and border crossing encouraged a critical reflection of the border by young artistic movements in Tijuana between the mid-nineties and the early 21st century.

Challenging a then-trending view of Tijuana as a synthetic "hybrid" and product of semiotic "fusion" of bipolar, disparate Mexican and American cultures, writer Heriberto Yépez, one of the main intellectual figures in Tijuana, claimed that "the border and its aesthetics are not defined by its synthesis but by its contradictions", and that "'fusion' as metaphor would only hide inequalities, and what defines border is precisely its inequalities" (Yépez, 2005: 34, 18).

At the turn of the century, the border became, for Tijuana's young media artists (most of them coming from the middle class), a social as well as a material condition they wanted sometimes surpassed and erased, sometimes critically assumed and exposed. Asserting and suspicious of globality and "glocal" celebratory discourses, the border is a permanent conflicting multidimensional site that gives advantages to young artists to connect with people, international circuits, and technologies, although within a daily experience of marginality, subalternity, and precariousness. How is this complex production of identities by young movements that started to promote digital culture and multimedia experimentalism in Tijuana in the early 2000 to be tackled? What does digital culture allow as a distinct form of activism in the local context, and to what extent does it contribute to border critical thinking?

With this in mind, this chapter shows how artists reflect and position themselves in relation to border experiences and through digital media, from hacktivism strategies that connect them to other activist media groups in the United States, to the development of open-source platforms from which they can link to centers of media artistic development directly related to Silicon Valley.

This research considers the complex cultural play that Mexican artists perform themselves as border subjects, constantly exceeding a binary structure of representation in order to re-site boundaries (Hall, 1990), which also means to "engage cultural and social constructs in complex ways that equally resist and reinforce aspects of hegemonic culture" (Madrid, 2008: 8). As we shall see, the colonial experience is not primarily an external force, but also a formative aspect of continuous becoming of identity.

This study is based on online research, as well as interviews that were part of a broader ethnographic research, to cast the assemblage between actors, discourses, technologies, and institutions of electronic scenes in the Tijuana–San Diego border.

Based on Bruno Latour's *Actor-Network-Theory* (Latour, 2005), and Benjamin Piekut's *ANT* application to explain formations of New York experimentalism during the 1960s (Piekut, 2011), the study of an actor network has allowed to tackle how border and media experimentalism at the turn of the century have been interrelated and performed by some Tijuana-based artists. Thus, this study is framed by digital diasporas studies as these "acknowledge digital diasporas . . . constituted here and there, through bodies and data, across borders and networks, online and offline, by users and platforms, through material, symbolic, and emotional practices that are all reflective of intersecting power relations" (Candidatu *et al.*, 2019: 34).

Mix Media Art and Cyberactivism for Border Thinking

Backgrounds of interdisciplinarity, multimedia, and border art date back to the mid-1980s, through initiatives such as the bi-national Border Art Workshop/Taller de Arte Fronterizo (BAW/TAF), cofounded by artist David

Avalos together with performer artists such as Guillermo Gómez-Peña under the sponsorship of the Centro Cultural de la Raza, San Diego. Experiences, thoughts, theory, and all kinds of visual and acoustic evidence were gathered in many formats (particularly installation and performance) in order to talk about the Tijuana–San Diego border from both sides. It was later in the 1990s that artists, in the context of Internet rising as a communication network, and a site for "direct action" and political resistance (particularly through the example of Zapatistas movement), that groups of artists and activists joined with electronic actions. Some of them included website mass blockades to government, financial, and other hegemonic power institutions, with the argument that current mobile, immaterial, and nomadic forms of capital through electronic networks should also be the main site for activism and political struggle. Founded in 1997 by artist and programmer Ricardo Domínguez, *Electronic Disturbance Theater* was a cyberactivist group aimed at creating electronic tools[2] and actions against the Mexican and US governments; in response, both governments (particularly the Secretaría de Gobernación and United States Department of Defense) provoked counterattacks to the Flood-Net user's Internet browser in 1998.

Electronic networks and media as a new dimension for critical theory were used to expand nomadic resistance actions in both countries, calling people beyond geographic borders to act for specific territories, pointing out concrete racial and material exclusions. These actions with and across borders connected Domínguez and the Electronic Disturbance Theater with Tijuana-based artist Fran Illich.

In the mid-1990s, Illich joined other artists—including Gabriel Trujillo Muñoz, José Luis Ramírez, and Luis Humberto Rosales—to create the Cinemátik collective. Moving around local fanzine projects related to punk bands, graffiti and comics, video, cinema, and the electronic music independent scene, they sought to connect underground local expressions (raves and alternative narratives of the city told by media artists groups like *Los culturosos* or *La family*) to other digital political movements that were almost absent not only in Tijuana, but in Mexican contemporary visual and digital art.

The Cinemátik collective was inspired by a mix of techno subcultures like British Spiral Tribe, digital studies, *net.art* figures such as Natalie Bookchin and Alexei Shulgin, and American groups promoting tactical media-based actions[3] such as RTMark,[4] Critical Art Ensemble,[5] Electronic Disturbance Theater's hacktivism, or the Department of Art and Technology,[6] just to mention a few.

An outcome of this mix of cyberculture and hacktivism, Cinemátik 1.0, was, according to Illich, one of the first festivals of its kind in Latin America. Held in 1998, this event established links and a conceptual framework for two later initiatives: net net net mx fest and Borderhack.

Borderhack was inspired in media theorist and curator Florian Schneider's bordercamps—meetings of artists, activists, and hackers along European borders who worked during a week in critical border interventions—as part of the anti-racist network initiative *Kein Mensch ist Illegal*,[7] founded at the Documenta X Art exhibition in Berlin in 1997. According to Illich, "Borderhack was both, a physical and virtual attack against that border wall through mass media", which he related to graffiti interventions by collectives Hecho en México and Decorando la Ciudad in symbolic sites such as San Ysidro's checkpoint.[8]

To what extent would digital "disobedience" approaches reveal new aspects of concrete border experiences, i.e., its underlying power dynamics? Is hacking more than a metaphor of border artistic interventions? If hacking were conceived only as a way to "damage" hegemonic power or symbolic and material infrastructure, then artists would pretend the existence of a binary opposition (us/them) performed only from a fixed subaltern position. However, the Borderhack Manifesto claims that

> hacking is understood as the penetration, exploration or investigation of a system with the goals of understanding it, not of destroying it, and that is exactly what we are trying to do: to understand the border, to know what it represents and to become aware of the role that we play in it. All this with the goal of improving the relations between two worlds (the first and the third), Mexico and the US . . . by doing it right at the physical border, . . . to get to the bottom of the problem and really understand what is it that unites us and what is it that separates us.[9]

Borderhack was a tactical way to reveal border contradictions: using technological infrastructure with the help of international artists to stress social inequalities between the "two worlds"; for instance, in collaboration with Electronic Disturbance Theater and Ricardo Domínguez, they hacked the Border Patrol's website using FloodNet software, targeting the Mexican government as "the enemy", for "it has allowed poverty come too far".[10] By doing actions during Borderhack camping days, like repeatedly crossing the borderline in front of Border Patrol—thus ironically performing a sort of "cops and robbers" game—border was being dialectically vanished and confirmed. As scholar Rita Raley points out:

> border represents . . . a space of exclusion that is haunted by the return of that which it has to exclude over and over again. This is to say; the border is what becomes spectralized by the very return of the migrant. The border, then, functions as a space that is both real and yet made unreal.
> (Raley, 2009: 40)

Borderhack's discourse considers social asymmetry as a fundamental aspect of border relationships:

> This is the border. Our border. A place where we earn pesos and consume in dollars. Where we live almost in the US. Where we can smell the future coming from the freeways, from Silicon Valley, from Hollywood, but yet we are trapped in a muddy hill with unpaved streets. . . . The border is unilateral, only when going from Mexico to the US. The other way around is a free zone. . . . The wall is "one way".[11]

Media and symbolic infrastructure at the Cinemátik 1.0 festival was sponsored by an international web of hackers who provisionally installed a Border Radio with free independent telephone lines to connect families in distant places between Mexico and the US; FloodNet-based cyber-actions massively blocked the Border Patrol's website; and a special essays column in *Wired News* clearly showed that this festival was far from just playing a marginalized position, particularly in the context of hacktivism and international media art trends. Furthermore, it was also avant-garde media counterculture trends in Global North by that time that nurtured the idea of hacking; so, the more attractive this was for Mexican border artists, and the more they attempted as hackers to penetrate the border "to discover its workings", the more they demonstrated and performed its contradictions; a contradictory flowing state of colonial subjectivity.

This complex relation to and construction of border was two-sided, as borderhacking became a necessary performance for Chicano artists and other collectives critical of US institutions and border policies.

Between the years of Borderhack fest edition (2000–2002), RTMark, Electronic Disturbance Theater, San Diego–based Taco Shop Poets, and the US Department of Art and Technology participated in media pranks, public border art interventions, and counter-information tactics. For example, the US Department of Art and Technology's "secretary" once mailed Borderhack's organizers with an offer "to open frontier in [Borderhack's] camping area, allowing people to freely circulate during three days, as a symbolic act".[12] On the other hand, Electronic Disturbance Theater's preparation of a cyber blockade against the Border Patrol's site was included in a record of attacks targeting various institutions and symbols of Mexican and American neoliberalism: NAFTA, CAFTA, the School for the Americas, and the US Defense Department, among others (see Raley, 2009: 40). On these interventions by tactical media artists, author Raley infers

> a strange relation between the material border and network traffic, between flooding a material border and flooding a server. Flooding,

pulsing, "apparent inexhaustibility"—this [she sustains] is the mode of the swarm, the paradigmatic mode of conflict for netwar and for the Electronic Disturbance Theater.

(Raley, 2009: 40)

Temporary, nomadic, virtually distributed, and offline, physical and anonymous actions on the border produce multi-layered, dynamical comprehensions of it, resulting in fluid productions of *unequal* multiple identities that simultaneously acknowledge both social asymmetries and an internal colonialism while overturning binarisms in a new way. On the side of Tijuana, this relationship could be interpreted following Stuart Hall's questions in his paradigmatic text *Cultural Identity and Diaspora*:

> The dialogue of power and resistance, of refusal and recognition with and against *Presence Europeene* . . . is always-already fused, syncretized with other cultural elements. . . . How can we stage this dialogue so that, finally, we can place it, without terror or violence, rather than being forever placed by it? Can we ever recognize its irreversible influence, whilst resisting its imperialistic eye?"

(Hall, 1990: 233)

Network Culture and Open-source based Artistic Movements for Tijuana Border Hacking

Besides hacktivism as a distinct form of straight political action, digital culture was also reflected by border Mexican artists as a condition for establishing knowledge communities and production modes based on network-distributed authorship. Since the end of the 1990s, artists began to join in free-culture movement through the intrinsic possibilities of digital technologies to easily copy, distribute, remix, improve, and update hardware, code, and media contents, thus adopting new forms of producing, developing, sharing artistic processes, technologies, and knowledge under copy-left and free licenses bolstered by digital context (Ottavi, 2008: 29). By doing this, artists have deliberately challenged, or at least softened, privatization of culture and capitalist modes of production that seek to control knowledge and culture through copyright restrictions. Since rising use of the Internet in the early 2000s, global free and open-source movement have allowed young Tijuana artists to negotiate marginal border conditions with imaginaries of the on- and offline mediascape in order to link "multiple subject positions", as scholar Homi Bhabha suggests (1994: 245). Co-produced and co-distributed digital tools and artworks as a special sort of "diasporic media" enable certain ways of co-presence among geographically distant individuals, and as authors Tsagarousianou and Retis maintain, this provides "the opportunity of producing new spaces where multiple remote localities and the experiences generated and shared by their inhabitants come together and become synchronized and related to each-other" (Tsagarousianou and Retis, 2019: 5). This type of distributed production of artistic work, identity, and space was strategic for Tijuana-based artists in the 2000s as they experienced precarious local conditions daily. This is the case of mid-80s–born artist Leslie García and the collective Dream Addictive, which will be discussed next.

After leaving a career in design at Universidad de Baja California, García moved to Tijuana in 2003 where she met Carmen González and Alejandro Ramírez, with whom she co-founded the Dream Addictive media art collective. It was inspired by the open-source interactive, and '90s net.art movement that, following pioneer artists Alexei Shulgin and Natalie Bookchin, had initially encouraged "independence from institutional bureaucracies, . . . whereby an artist/individual could be equal to and on the same level as any institution or corporation . . . [to realize] [t]he practical death of the author" (Shulgin and Bookchin, 1999).

By 2000, net.art claims had been put in question due to its inclusion in the dynamics of contemporary art institutions. Nevertheless, in the context of Tijuana, achieving empowering independence through net based art was, for local artists, still feasible. So, according to García,

> producing work for the web . . . [gave us] empowerment, for we didn't need a gallery, nor a [institutional] representation, nor a fixed space to communicate what we were thinking in that moment, aside from having the scope that we had by doing this for the web. There was a tangible force, as the collective was suddenly known in many places. Through it I met most of the people that I know nowadays.[13]

By such affirmation we can infer that producing web-based works does not necessarily perform a counter-cultural political positioning or counter-cultural hacktivism for these artists. Rather, as this case shows, it might be a strategy to deal with the lack of exhibition spaces in Tijuana. Digital free-culture was claimed by Dream Addictive as a response to concrete situated conditions. In a place lived as "precarious and unfavorable", where collaboration and participation is not so much a poetic idea but rather "a survival issue",[14] network platforms were an imperative, not an option.

Internet-based art and digital art networks such as Turbulence and Net-worked Performance[15] gave Dream Addictive a sense of "ubiquity", an actively coproduced mediascape to perform "multiple subject positions", whereby they could work and imagine border dissolution. García relates this operation to a "hacker" positioning of border thinking, in contrast with Cinemátik's understanding of borderhack, as they were not intending to delete border—i.e., its inherent asymmetries, disagreement, and contradictions—but rather "to apply to it a little reverse engineering, in other words, to try to understand its structure and to discover its workings."[16]

In addition to strategic involvement with the global free and open-source movement, groups like Dream Addictive benefited from geographical proximity to San Diego, having access not only to audio and video technologies, but also to high-tech technology centers and scholars. They established contact with artists and researchers like Amy Alexander, Eduardo Navas, and Miller Puckette, who worked in the fields of digital art, computer music, remix theory, and media culture for the California Institute of the Arts, San Diego State University, and the University of California at San Diego.

Given the proximity to the Silicon Valley region, such material and symbolic capital networks allowed Dream Addictive to link their artistic development to electronic design with international tech festivals in California; particularly ZERO1: The Art and Technology Network and the ZERO1 Biennial, Build Your Own World.

Founded in 2000 in Silicon Valley, ZERO1 dated back to high-tech marketing pioneer Andy Cunningham, the same figure "who had been instrumental to the success of companies such as Apple, Cisco, and HP".[17] With the goal "to bring artists and technologists together" and "to encourage creativity at the intersection of art and technology", ZERO1 became a reference within "the 'business incubator' model made popular by Silicon Valley's technology and start-up companies", from which the American Arts Incubator program, supported by the US State Department's Bureau of Educational and Cultural Affairs, emerged.

The ZERO1 Biennial was organized as an artist showcase with over 100 artists, designers, engineers, filmmakers, musicians, architects, and avant-garde creators from 21 countries in order to encourage innovation in social issues through technological infrastructure and "trans-cultural idea exchange" as well.

The Dream Addictive collective participated in the third edition of the Biennial in 2010, presenting the Open Solar Circuits project, developed in the same year and commissioned by Medialab Prado Madrid. Such a project was based upon collaborative creation of a virtual public-access repository, aimed to store and systematize knowledge on the development and design of sustainable energy-driven electronic circuits, especially those powered by solar energy. This virtual platform was inspired by the idea of "framework", "a standardized set of concepts, practices, and criteria focusing a particular kind of issues that serve as a referent to address and solve new similar problems"[18], useful in software development, management systems, and computing applications. In this case, the Open Solar Circuits framework was shaped by circuit designs and tutorials chosen by collaborators of the Medialab Prado Madrid project according to its feasibility. It was intended that any person interested could build those circuits from scratch by herself, as well as share developments and enhancements through the same repository using open-source applications, such as Fritzing for circuit design and prototyping, or Github for programming code sharing.

The idea of framework as workflow structure and tool objectivation for circuit development is based upon the idea of replication, adaptation, and knowledge transfer that exceeds any geographical limitations, adapting content to local conditions of use and reuse while keeping a structural translocal basis.

As a precarious reality and as a strategic bridge with the Global North, Dream Addictive fostered a "framework" development supported by the tools and terms of the digital era as an instance of border critical thinking, i.e., as a way to renegotiate "multiple subject positions", as scholar Homi Bhabha points out.

Beyond a platform for sharing creative tools and ideas, the Open Solar Circuits "framework" operates as an infrastructure for rearticulation, displacement, and redistribution of subjectivities that could be described using Stuart Hall's pondering on the so called "New World":

> The Third, "New World" presence, is not so much power, as ground, place, territory. It is the juncture-point where the many cultural tributaries meet . . . where strangers from every other part of the globe collided. None of the people who now occupy the islands . . . originally "belonged" there. It is the space where the creolization and assimilations and syncretisms were negotiated. . . . It also has to be understood as the place of many, continuous displacements.
>
> (Hall, 1990: 234)

Conclusions

Although artistic practices that emerged from border and digital culture could easily subscribe a neoliberal discourse based on frontier permeability for free cultural capital exchange and a "conciliation of despaired codes and practices on a common exotic space" (Yépez, 2005: 12), the cases previously discussed show how a geopolitical point of view determines the way of conceiving space and forms of interaction inside digital environments. In the case of Fran Illich and the Cinemátik collective, hacktivism permits the expansion of strategies and spaces to denounce social inequality as a border inherent condition, as well as stressing the inherent contradictions of a subjectivity embodying contra-cultural references and tactics of Global

North-born media art, in order to affirm artists' position as colonial subjects, while recognizing themselves as forerunners of the Latin American cyberculture movement of their time.

Inequality or opposition between cultural binarisms are not overcome by any of the digital platforms or strategies explored by the aforementioned artists. Rather, these strategies aim at putting into question narratives that limit them to occupy a fixed position as subaltern or marginal subjects facing the Global North. Digitality enables them to accomplish tactical actions with and across borders. Artists underline the effects that sociopolitical and territorial concrete borders produce on them; nevertheless, they are able to perform virtual border crossings by working with shared, distributed, and sometimes anonymous production of tools for network artistic creation and online activism.

Permeable, ambiguous, multiple borders finally constitute themselves as sites of dialogue between power and resistance, from electronic art movements in such conflictive frontier spaces as Tijuana, that call for powerful narratives on diaspora and displacement of digital identities, as well as critical artistic thinking around the reinforcement of bio-political and material borders inside current digital mediascapes.

Notes

1. Background to the Office of the Inspector General Investigation. https://oig.justice.gov/special/9807/gkp01.htm
2. They created a device called FloodNet that "took the form of a Java applet that allowed users to send useless requests or personalized messages to a remote web server in a coordinated fashion, thereby slowing it down and filling its error logs with words of protest and gibberish—a kind of virtual sit-in". https://anthology.rhizome.org/floodnet
3. A term coined in 1996, tactical media is an artistic approach grounded in media appropriation and intervention tactics. Politicians' and corporations' web sites, official newscasts, and mass-consumption advertising are interfered with as sites of political and economic order by transmitting counter-information through these very communication channels, thus provoking destabilization of their public image and symbolic order. Dutch researcher Geert Loving was one of the leading figures in theorizing the tactical media concept and movement, creating the Institute of Network Cultures in 2004.
4. RTMark. http://archive.rhizome.org/artbase/1693/index.html
5. Critical Art Ensemble. http://critical-art.net/
6. US Department of Art and Technology. www.usdat.us/
7. Kein Mensch ist Illegal. www.kein-mensch-ist-illegal.org/
8. Fran Illich, *De cómo vencimos el miedo y decidimos jugar con la frontera: Borderhack.* www.jornada.com.mx/2003/10/12/mas-fran.html
9. Fran Illich & Luis Humberto Rosales, *Borderhack 2000.* http://subsol.c3.hu/subsol_2/contributors/ilichtext.html
10. Illich, *op. cit.*

11. Illich & Rosales, *op. cit.*
12. Illich, *op. cit.*
13. Personal communication with Leslie García. Mexico City. May 2, 2014.
14. *Ibid.*
15. The Networked_Performance blog was created in 2004 by Jo-Anne Green and Helen Thorington of Turbulence.org, and Michelle Riell, Assistant Professor of New Media at California State University Monterey Bay. The idea behind the blog was "to chronicle current network-enabled practice, to obtain a wide-range of perspectives on issues and to uncover commonalities in the work", by using "the continuing advances in internet technologies, wireless telecommunications, sensor technologies and Geographic Information Systems". Turbulence. http://turbulence.org/blog/about/
16. Illich & Rosales, *op. cit.*
17. Zero, *The Art & Technology Network.* https://zero1.org/support/leader
18. Framework. https://es.wikipedia.org/wiki/Framework

References

Bhabha, H. (1994). *The Location of Culture.* New York: Routledge.

Candidatu, L., Leurs K., & Ponzanesi S. (2019). "Digital Diasporas: Beyond the Buzzword: Toward a Relational Understanding of Mobility and Connectivity". In *The Handbook of Diasporas, Media, and Culture* (eds. Jessica Retis & Roza Tsagarousianou). Hoboken, NJ: John Wiley & Sons. 31–48.

Hall, S. (1990). "Cultural Identity and Diaspora". In *Identity: Community, Culture, Difference.* London: Lawrence & Wishart. 222–237.

Latour, B. (2005). *Reassembling the Social: An Introduction to Actor-Network-Theory.* New York: Oxford University Press.

Madrid, A. L. (2008). *Nor-Tec Rifa! Electronic Dance Music from Tijuana to the World.* New York: Oxford University Press.

Ottavi, J. (2008). "The 'Free' and New Creative Practices: Open Source Modular Artefacts". In *FLOSS+ Art.* France: GOTO10. 28–33.

Piekut, B. (2011). *Experimentalism Otherwise: The New York Avant-Garde and Its Limits.* Berkeley: University of California Press.

Raley, R. (2009). *Tactical Media.* Minneapolis: University of Minnesota Press.

Shulgin, A., & Bookchin, N. (1999). *Introduction to Net Art (1994–1999).* www.easylife.org/netart/

Tsagarousianou, R., & Retis, J. (2019). "Diasporas, Media, and Culture: Exploring Dimensions of Human Mobility and Connectivity in the Era of Global Interdependency". In *The Handbook of Diasporas, Media, and Culture* (eds. Jessica Retis & Roza Tsagarousianou). Hoboken, NJ: John Wiley & Sons. 1–20.

Yépez, H. (2005). *Made in Tijuana.* Mexicali: Instituto de Cultura de Baja California.

3 Sonic Borders of Self

A Trajectory

Wilfrido Terrazas

I

The ways in which our mature creative work can be affected by the experiences from our formative years are, I find, a fascinating topic. Often, we find ourselves unconsciously trying to answer old questions, solve old riddles, overcome old hurdles. Allow me to provide an example. In a recent interview by Frank J. Oteri, the great American pianist, improviser, and composer Myra Melford was asked if she considered whether her early studies in environmental sciences had had an impact on her music. Melford replied that she had been interested in many things growing up, and that she wasn't sure. Oteri then reminded her that, even if her music is not "overtly political or overtly environmental", she does name all her groups, and "all of those names are actually things that refer back to nature". An acute observation that must have thrown her off a bit, because she then responded: "Wow, I never thought about that. Well there you go. See, I guess it is important to me. But it's certainly not conscious".[1] As I was reading this, I couldn't help suspecting that the presence of nature in Melford's work is akin to that of the border in my own. Both are almost ever present, but perhaps unnoticeable for most listeners, including ourselves, the artists, supposedly in control. In my performances and compositions as well as in my teaching, I am always crossing borders. I am referring here to the rather imaginary borders that, in our minds, separate concepts such as composition, improvisation, and performance; events planned and unplanned; melody and shape; heterophony and polyphony; pulse, in particular its repetition, evolution, and denial; musical genres and traditions, especially within the huge umbrella that encompasses experimental/improvised/new music; being "in the moment" versus perceiving "the whole picture"; musical time(s); and many more. In recent years, I began to understand how all those assumed oppositions work in the music I do, but, for the longest time, I didn't know they were relevant, and, even when I started realizing they were, I had no idea how. In this chapter, I will try to retrace the presence of the border in my work, with the hopes of finding its trajectory. For that effect, I will visit several stages of my artistic life and, though the journey will most certainly be non-linear, I am hoping the trajectory it draws will be clear and eloquent enough to show the where, the how and, maybe, the why, it is at the center of my creative practice.

The border between Mexico and the United States has been a major point of reference my whole life. It has always been there, as an unavoidable presence I have had to negotiate with countless times. For years I have thought that growing up near the border shapes people in a very particular way. I grew up in the Mexican city of Ensenada, Baja California, located roughly a hundred kilometers south of the Tijuana–San Diego border, by the Pacific coast. I didn't grow up right by the border, but I did visit Tijuana with my family very often as a kid and spend most holidays there. We would cross the border into San Diego mostly to go shopping. It was a different world back then. Crossing was easier and a lot faster. It was a normal part of the lives of many Mexican families of the border regions (it clearly still is). One would cross to shop for groceries, clothes, gadgets, Christmas gifts. I had a couple of aunts who would cross every Sunday to do their laundry. Having crossed the border all my life, I am very familiar with the culture around it: what to expect, what to say and when, what to do, what not to do. I believe the act of crossing them is the essence of all borders. Regardless of nationalities or migratory status, we who cross the border, make it. We define it. It is our border. They hold it. They draw the line. But the cultural significance and the complexity of meanings (dare I say its poetics?) that are the border are ours, and they are powerful identity markers indeed.

II

I discovered music when I was 12 years old, but it was only after I started playing the flute, at age 15, that I realized it was something I wanted to do for the rest of my life. In 1990, just before turning 16, I started taking flute lessons at the Centro de Estudios Musicales of the Universidad Autónoma de Baja California[2] in Ensenada. The story that I would like to tell begins two years later, around the time when I graduated from high school,[3] in the spring of 1992. One very fortunate day, my friend Álvaro Díaz[4] and I attended a concert of the San Diego Youth Symphony[5] in Tijuana's CECUT.[6] We were utterly impressed by the near-professional quality of the performance and, back in Ensenada, we talked to everybody we knew about it. Our friend and mentor Ernesto Rosas[7] then suggested that we audition and join the orchestra, which I initially thought was way out of our possibilities. Fortunately, Álvaro disagreed with me and crossed to San Diego the next weekend with his oboe. He presented a simple audition and got accepted into the orchestra. Encouraged by his success, I followed suit the week after that. I also got in. That was the very first time I got to play with colleagues from the other side of the border. I was 17. Even though I played with the San Diego Youth Symphony only for a few months, the experience was mind blowing. In sharp contrast to anything we had known before, this was a real symphony orchestra, and its members were remarkably proficient players. Furthermore, most of these kids were not even aspiring to become professional musicians, which to us was simply unbelievable. We had stumbled upon a completely different reality.

The San Diego Youth Symphony experience, though brief, proved to be key for the developments that followed. In October of 1992, I found myself without a flute teacher, as the teacher I had been studying with for a year and half suddenly left Baja California. Following Ernesto's advice once more, I spoke with one of my colleagues from the Youth Symphony and asked her for her teacher's phone number. She had, I later found out, a locally well-known and prestigious teacher. His name was Damian Bursill-Hall, and at the time he was Principal Flutist with both the San Diego Symphony Orchestra and the San Diego Opera. Damian was my first real flute teacher. He was brilliant and experienced, but also kind and generous. I remember he would charge his American students a fee of $40 per hour, but he would charge me only $25 (and our lessons often went on for more than an hour).[8] He had a very structured approach to flute pedagogy, one that learned deeply from both the French and the American flute traditions, but he had somehow synthesized them, creating an original approach. He had a major influence on my playing and my teaching, and I continue to learn from him after all these years. Early in 1993, I moved to Tijuana, where I took music theory and history classes, plus sang in a choir and played lots of chamber music as a student of the Talleres de la Orquesta de Baja California program.[9] In those years my average week would include crossing the border three or four times. I would take flute lessons with Damian, attend concerts, participate in masterclasses, festivals, and orchestral summer programs, and, above all, visit bookstores and libraries. I would also spend most weekends teaching in Ensenada. Commuting between the three cities became an important component of my life, one that I would come back to twice in later years. It was also around this time that I basically taught myself to speak English. My parents spoke only Spanish, and, even though I did learn some basic English at school, I realized right from the first rehearsal at the Youth Symphony, and especially at my first flute lesson with Damian, that my knowledge of the English language was very limited. But living the life of the border paid off. I was rapidly becoming a better flutist and a better musician, was doing so in two languages and, at the same time, I was getting a glimpse into a reality completely different from the one I knew and had grown up in. It was an intense formative experience, which I believe marked me for life.

It was around this time when I also met Claire Chase.[10] We became the closest of friends right away. When I met her in 1993–94, she was already a phenomenal player. It was through her that I came to understand American culture much better. We would recommend each other books and music and write each other long letters. She helped me improve my English, and I encouraged her to learn Spanish. I recommended she study with Damian, which she did; and she would tell me about her early studies with John Fonville, who years later became my teacher. Claire is super famous now, but the first international concert of her career was a flute duo recital which we played together in Ensenada, in December of 1995. Over the years, we have continued to collaborate occasionally and always ask each other for advice on important matters pertaining both flute playing and life. The story of our friendship, which I guess will have to be told in detail elsewhere, sums up what the border means to me: Once upon a time, there were two kids who played the flute on either side of the border. They met and became friends for life. They decided to make music together and learn from each other, as equals, in spite of everything.

In the summer of 1996, I moved to Morelia, a beautiful city in Western Mexico, to study at the Conservatorio de las Rosas. After I graduated in 2000, I moved back to Ensenada for two and a half years, and my life between three cities reactivated. During that time, I would cross the border at least once a month to take lessons from John Fonville, who at the time was the flute professor at the University of California, San Diego. John was a great mentor, and he helped me figure so many things out. I saw John as a pioneer and legendary figure in the kind of flute playing I was interested in, and I admired him greatly. He also proved to be an immensely wise and generous person, and I am so grateful to have been his student. Furthermore, UCSD has always been a very special place for me. I used to spend countless hours at Geisel Library, getting to know so much music, and attend concerts at the Music Department there. In 1995, I heard John play a concert and decided I had to study with him at some point. It was my dream to study at UCSD. The dream, however, never really materialized, but it was perhaps better that way. Still, I got to be John's private student between 2000 and 2003, before moving to Mexico City, where I was based for 14 and a half years.

III

It is such a curious thing that I began to understand what the border meant to me in the years I lived far from it. Since this not the place to tell my Mexico City story, let me just say that it was a very hard experience moving there, and that it took me years to get things going. But, in the long run, being based in such a massive cultural hub as Mexico City is what allowed me to build something resembling an artistic career playing new/experimental/ improvised music. This section of the chapter is not about that, though. Not really. What I want to talk about here is a certain inner conflict, one that took me a long time to even notice, much less comprehend. I want to tell the story of my inner sonic "borders" and how I managed to understand them, in order to use them creatively. So, let us briefly go back to 1992, that pivotal year I was describing before. It was that year that I improvised in public for the first time, as I joined a group of friends in providing live music for a dance project in Ensenada (this was also my first interdisciplinary project ever, and my first experience in collective creation, even though I of course didn't realize any of that).[11] That same year, I started writing my first composition, a very naive chamber piece for oboe, bassoon, and strings, which I finished at some point in 1993.[12] Finally, also in 1993, I performed a world premiere for the first time.[13] In spite of the fact that these three life-defining events happened around the same time, I didn't seem to make a connection between them. They involved a lot of the same abilities, people, and places, but, somehow, from the start, improvising, composing, and performing new works were three completely different, unrelated processes in my mind. For years they remained so. I felt the need of somehow bringing them together, but I didn't know how. I could not cross those borders. Between 1993 and 2006, I was mostly focused on performing, although I never gave up on the other two. I wrote very few compositions in those years, always seriously doubting if I really wanted to compose. On the other hand, I would improvise often, but seldom in public. In my first years in Mexico City, this fundamental disconnect between my three main artistic activities was already a serious conflict. I felt unbalanced, unsatisfied, and untrue to my calling, which, I realize now, was completely unclear to me. At the time, I was performing lots of new works, most of them written for me by young Mexican composers. Many of those pieces were great, and I enjoyed playing them, but it was clear to me that I was not finding in them what I was looking for.

Things started going in the right direction in 2006, for two reasons. Firstly, because of the foundation of the Mexico City–based improvisers collective Generación Espontánea, a project which continues to exist against all odds. GE came about in a crucial moment of emergence of the experimental music scene in Mexico City and provided an exciting platform that allowed me to finally focus on improvising in a much more serious way. Secondly, because I started to realize that I did wanted to compose, and I began writing music in a more conscious, goal-oriented, and disciplined way. Each piece I wrote in the years between 2006 and 2012 explored ideas and approaches to notation whose general aim was to open interpretative possibilities. In other words, and I realized this only years later, I had started writing compositions that explored different ways of transferring the power of decision making to the performers.

In the compositions from said period, the first thing I did was get rid of all traces of rigorously notated rhythm. Notated rhythm has always bothered me. It is so inflexible. Once you notate rhythm, that's it, it cannot be changed. It is true it can be interpreted in many ways, but its identity remains fixed forever, and I wanted to explore other alternatives. In pieces like *Ariete* (2006–07), for flute, clarinet, guitar, and percussion, or *A String Set* (2008–09), for any bowed string instrument, I explored a pulse-based proportional notation, which gave performers a certain amount of flexibility that I thought was interesting. It was a first step. Around the same time, eager to allow performers to improvise in my pieces, I also began exploring two kinds of text scores. On the one hand, there's the "set of instructions" approach, which I used in pieces like *Varesiana* (2006), for open ensemble; *Into White Tunnels of Wind* (2007), for any wind instrument and radio; and, later, in *The Split Trilogy* (2011–12).[14] And, on the other hand, and probably the most fruitful exploration of the period, was the writing of text scores in a timeline, in pieces like *Heterofonía Ia (para G.L.)* (2007), for flute and fixed media, and, especially, *Mosquito War Grooves* (2009), for open ensemble. The latter opened very interesting possibilities up, but it still featured the use of specific time frames to allow a stopwatch-guided performance, which I later felt was just too constraining. So, in the next open ensemble piece I wrote, *Retrato de Walter Lärmer* (2011–12), I set out to open the possibilities even more, and proposed the idea of "mobile temporality" which in recent scores I have explained thus:

> The total duration is not determined by the composer, since the temporality of the piece is mobile. This means that, in rehearsals and/or in performance, the performers should look for the temporality with which they feel most at ease with, as if trying to find a hidden oral tradition of the piece.[15]

Going through the process of finding their own temporality, the performers (re)build the piece to fit their abilities and expressive possibilities. I came up with this simple idea by observing how musicians in many folk music traditions work new versions of old repertoire out, a process that has fascinated me for a long time. I reversed this process and started asking myself: What if we were to play new pieces as if they were old? Is it possible to imagine a hidden, hypothetical, oral tradition of a new or very recent piece? Such is the whole idea of mobile temporality. *Retrato de Walter Lärmer* was my first piece with no specific time frames, no stopwatches or conductors, and no fixed proportionality. In my composed music, temporality had become a responsibility of the performers.

IV

Retrato de Walter Lärmer is a successful piece in several ways: It is very easy to perform, even by ensembles with little improvising experience; it's fun, engaging, practical, and clear. But, I realized quickly, there was still one major challenge that text scores, even ones as free as *Retrato*, do not seem to surpass, which is the fact that after three or four attempts, most performers tend to fixate things and improvise less and less. This comes naturally with repetition and is a common fact in working with open scores in general. This conundrum was one of several reasons that led me to propose the idea of "growth modules", which have become central to most of my recent compositions, but, before I explain what they are, I need to go back once more to the early 1990s.

This time I am going back even further, to the time when I started playing the flute, during the spring of 1990. I had been listening to jazz for a year or so, fascinated by that music, which had not been a part of my childhood's musical landscape. I discovered it completely by chance. In my early teens, I had been listening to The Beatles. My parents had one of those LP box collections people used to order through the mail back then. One day, at a local supermarket in Ensenada, I saw a record containing Beatles songs covered by jazz artists. It was inexpensive and I bought it. It blew my mind. Eventually, I started looking for records which featured flutists, and that's how I discovered Latin jazz. When I decided to enroll in flute lessons that was the music I wanted to learn. But nobody around was teaching that, and so I got sucked (gladly, but the verb is nonetheless fitting) into a long journey of classical training, followed by another long journey of new music training, which I already narrated in a rather succinct manner. But jazz stayed with me all that time. On the side, for my own personal interest, I would read through charts and try to imitate the style of playing I listened to in records. The Afro-Cuban style of flute playing interested me above all, and I was listening to great artists such as Orquesta Aragón, Irakere, Poncho Sánchez, or Cal Tjader with passion. The latter's album *La onda va bien*, which featured Roger Glenn's inimitable flute playing, was then, and still is, my favorite flute recording of all time.[16] I later discovered Coltrane and Eric Dolphy, Cecil Taylor, Ornette, Sun Ra, Don Cherry and, especially, the Art Ensemble of Chicago, which became a major inspiration. For the longest time, however, I could not find a way of bringing that world into my creative work. That started to change slowly in 2008, when I began collaborating with musicians with a jazz and rock background, and I realized how important African American music was to me.

My piece *Mosquito War Grooves*, mentioned already, was a first attempt in that direction. It's a very simple text score in a timeline which, among other things, asks the performers to collectively improvise grooves inspired by the African American tradition. Several others of my recent pieces have flirted with the idea of constructing a groove in different ways. But my clearest approximation has perhaps been the tunes I began writing in 2011. They are very simple, even silly, melodies that mostly compose themselves in my brain, sometimes in dreams, sometimes in semi-conscious situations. When I started writing them, I didn't really think they would be useful or interesting to explore at all, I just thought they were fun to play with. But they have proved to be very useful in recent years, providing very flexible structures to explore collective improvisation.

All of these explorations (text scores, mobile temporality, proportional notation, tune chart writing) were happening at the same time in my work when I met Roscoe Mitchell in October of 2011. Roscoe had been one of my longtime heroes and it was a dream of mine to meet him. So, when the opportunity arose of a residency at the Atlantic Center for the Arts in Florida to study and collaborate with him for three weeks, I didn't hesitate to apply. Fortunately, and along with a handful of amazing artists who became dear friends, I was selected to participate, and the residency turned out to be a wonderful, life-changing experience. Working with Roscoe helped me understand so many things that I would need to write another text just to tell that story. But I will say this: The illusory borders that I felt and struggled with in my creative practice were non-existent in Roscoe's. For him, there seemed to be no barriers between improvised and composed music, between a tradition and another, between one role and the others. He truly embodies the ideal of an integral artist which is inherent to most members of the AACM.[17]

V

A few months later, in the summer of 2012, and thanks to a grant from the Mexican government, I traveled to the Island of Kefalonia in Greece to carry out another residency, this time at the Ionion Center for the Arts and Culture. I was on my own, and I had two months to figure out once and for all what kind of music I wanted to write. The result was *Ítaca, viaje para un flautista*, a cycle of nine pieces for solo flute, which is easily my longest work so far, averaging 35–40 minutes when played in its entirety. Each of the pieces in *Ítaca* explores not only a particular flute sound world but also a particular way of allowing the performer to make decisions and improvise. Some familiar elements from older works can be found in *Ítaca*, but the central idea in it, one that appears for the first time, are growth modules, which in recent scores I have explained thus:

> *Growth Modules* . . . are platforms for improvisation. They contain certain material which acts as a *point of departure* to improvise, as the roots

of a rapidly growing plant (the stems, leaves and flowers do not necessarily resemble the roots, but they stem from them). The general idea is that the growth modules work in a similar way to how the improviser's memory would in a normal improvisation. Each letter, [in the score, depicts] a growth module, and they should be played in the given order (some material, or even entire sections can be, of course, left out). The order of the material within any given growth module can be changed at will, if desired. The verbal instructions at the beginning of the growth modules define their general musical character and give ideas for their interpretation.[18]

Growth modules are simply collections of musical material, notated mostly in conventional fashion, with some verbal (and, occasionally, graphic) elements from which performers take ideas to improvise. They are not expected to read the materials in order or to include all materials for that matter (although both are, of course, valid options). But they are expected to improvise with them. The possibilities of "growth" for these materials are as infinite as the possibilities of improvisation themselves, and each new performance has the potential to be very different from the last one (or the potential to be very similar!). I find that this fact reduces significantly the tendency of fixating things after a few attempts and encourages improvisation openly, keeping the score relevant and useful even if the piece has been played many times. Furthermore, what I found out after retraining myself in order to be able to perform this kind of score (a process which, by the way, was completely unexpected), was that the performer needs to bring themselves into it, they need to bring in their memory, their improvisation and interaction skills, their own personal sound world, but also their vulnerability, their unpreparedness, their doubts, because they don't really know where the journey is going to take them, and that is just the opposite of what we usually do in conventionally notated music, where we leave everything out except our relevant training and proceed to follow the composer's instructions. The idea of growth modules is obviously connected to Western modular notations and is somewhat influenced by the work of Mexican composer Ignacio Baca Lobera, with whom I have collaborated for many years. It also owes much to many traditions around the world, but the closest influence comes, clearly, from African American music. Jazz charts are treated by musicians basically as growth modules. The general idea is that everybody reads the same tune, but still manages to sound different from everyone else. Every new performance aims to be different from the previous ones. And, every tune retains their identity, regardless of the version or arrangement.

Most of my recent scores feature the use of growth modules and mobile temporality. They are performer-oriented devices; their nature is closer to that of maps than traditional scores. I provide an environment and certain flexible rules, but the performers create their own path through it. These pieces are therefore not "finished" in the conventional sense. They need the performers to enter them creatively, make decisions in real time, and figure them out. They are collaborative at their core. They are, above all, a means to an end. When they are performed, a new music emerges from the fusion of both our imaginations, a music that I could not have devised by myself. It took me years to understand that collaboration is what opens sonic borders. Most pieces I have composed since *Ítaca* are a response to a 20-year-old question of mine: What kind of music do I want to write? What I discovered in Greece was that my musical imagination is not very specific. I imagine global musical events, energy fluxes, contours, indomitable shapes, which for the most part do not show that many details in their behavior. They keep changing, refuse to be fixed. Some of my older pieces had lots of unnecessary information, stuff I was not really hearing. Writing that extra information was not only inaccurate, but a way of preventing other possible behaviors. I finally realized that what I hear are the possibilities of different behaviors, and only rarely specific ones. It took me a long time to understand that what I was interested in was the infinite possibilities of flow in music, and not in controlling it (or anyone).

VI

In recent years, I have continued to write music regularly, occasionally revisiting older explorations. *Luna de estambre* (2019), for two improvising soloists and open ensemble, for instance, learns from my previous experiences in writing text scores in a timeline. But most of my recent scores feature growth modules. My most ambitious project to date is the seven-piece *Torres* cycle, which I began writing in 2014 and hope to finish in 2020.[19] I have also continued to write tunes, which have proved valuable in developing several collaborative projects, especially the Ensenada-based Wilfrido Terrazas Sea Quintet.[20]

In 2014, I started a personal effort to reconnect with my home region. I joined forces with La Covacha Colectivo, a (then) three-people arts collective integrated by Julia Chávez Remigio, Esther Gámez Rubio, and Iván Trujillo, in founding the Semana de Improvisación La Covacha, now renamed Semana Internacional de Improvisación, a yearly week-long festival dedicated to improvised music in Ensenada. Julia quit the team after a few editions to focus on personal projects, but Esther, Iván, and myself have kept going and hope to continue the festival for years to come. The Semana has featured improvising artists from both sides of the border and beyond and is the only gathering of its kind in the region. In the most recent edition of the festival, in March 2019, we had support from UABC's Facultad de Artes, and we hope to keep growing. In recent years, I have also taught workshops and have been involved in several projects around Ensenada, Tijuana, and Mexicali. Unbeknownst to me, though, I was only laying the groundwork for bigger commitments.

By then, I had been wondering if it would be possible for me to leave Mexico City and return to my home region. In the summer of 2016, I found out that John Fonville was retiring, and that UC San Diego was looking to hire a new flute professor. At first, I didn't think I had a chance, but I was encouraged to apply by colleagues and friends, and so decided to try my luck. To my surprise, I made the short list, and eventually won the job. I still cannot believe it. In the fall of 2017, I moved to San Diego and started working at UCSD, where I have found a whole world of possibilities and a nurturing and supporting environment. Every day I arrive at my office and expect to wake up from a dream. It was my dream to study at UCSD, but I would never in a million years have dreamed about working there.[21] It's surreal. Life is certainly weird, and I realize that I may not be around for long, but since I started working at UCSD I thought that was all the more reason to spearhead, while I can, the creation of cross-border musical projects. My ongoing collaborations on the region go from Ensenada, coming through Tijuana and Mexicali, to San Diego, Orange County, and all the way up to Los Angeles. The more I reach out to people, the more of them are interested in making things happen. Now Ensenada also has a New Music Festival, led by fellow flutist Teresa Díaz, and many California-based guests have been featured at both that festival and at the Semana Internacional de Improvisación. Conversely, since my arrival, artists from Ensenada and Tijuana have been featured at UCSD concerts and events. My life as a cross-border artist has been reactivated once more, and this time I hope it will remain so. Looking forward, it all feels exciting.

I am a remarkably slow learner and it took me a long time to figure out what kind of music I really wanted to make, but the journey has been well worth it. Gradually, my inner borders have become blurry and porous. My current creative practice draws from my experience as a *fronterizo* in ways I could have never imagined, synthesizing old interests of mine that have been around since the beginning and many recent ones. I realize now that the physical and cultural borders of my home region relate intimately to the inner sonic borders of my musical practice: composing, improvising, performing, teaching, organizing, thinking/writing about music, etc., nurture each other inside and thus make more sense outside. All the struggles proved to be crucial. Every little failed experiment, every crossing attempt counted. Everything is important in the process of reconciling what was artificially divided: the what, the how, the why, and the where. Or, perhaps in this case, the why is the where. I understand now that I am supposed to be here, halfway. This trajectory is made of crossings. My where is in between.

Ensenada-San Diego, November 9–December 4, 2019

Notes

1. Frank J. Oteri, "Myra Melford: Freedom and Form", *New Music Box*, November 1, 2019. https://nmbx.newmusicusa.org/myra-melford-freedom-and-form/ (Accessed: November 10, 2019).
2. Baja California's public university, also known by the acronym UABC. The Centro de Estudios Musicales was established at the university in 1989 as a part of an extension program that included several artistic disciplines beside music. Much later, it became a part of the Escuela de Artes (now renamed Facultad de Artes), founded in 2003. Starting only then, the Facultad de Artes has offered a bachelor's degree (*licenciatura*) in music. It was the first institution in the State of Baja California to do so, and its first class graduated in 2007. See http://artes.ens.uabc.mx/index.php (Accessed: November 18, 2019).
3. Or, rather, the Mexican equivalent of high school, *bachillerato* or *preparatoria*.
4. He is one of the authors in this book. We are still collaborating after all these years!
5. According to their website, the San Diego Youth Symphony was founded in 1945 and "is the sixth oldest continuously operating youth orchestra in the United States and the resident youth orchestra in the City of San Diego's historic Balboa Park". See https://sdys.org/about/ (Accessed: November 17, 2019).
6. An acronym for the Centro Cultural Tijuana, a public institution founded in 1982, which is funded by the Mexican federal government and is probably the most important cultural hub in the city. See www.cecut.gob.mx/acerca.php (Accessed: November 17, 2019).
7. Born in 1951, pianist, composer, and conductor Ernesto Rosas Montoya has been a mentor to several generations of younger musicians in Ensenada. See Teresa Díaz de Cossío and Paul N. Roth's chapter in this book.
8. Years later, when I studied under John Fonville, he would also charge me only $25. I learned a valuable lesson in generosity from both. Incidentally, I remember this one time when John and I spoke about Damian, as we were discussing flute pedagogy approaches and different views on it. John had for Damian the greatest compliment I have ever heard from a flutist talking about another. He said: "Damian is his own flutist".
9. The program had changed its name to Programa Académico de la Orquesta de Baja California by the time I left it in 1996, and there have been several programs with different names in its stead ever since. The Orquesta de Baja California was founded in 1990 in Ensenada, as the first ever professional Western classical orchestra in the state. It changed its location to Tijuana in 1992. Throughout its existence, the OBC has oscillated between being an ensemble of soloists and a chamber orchestra. Currently, it is based at the Centro de Artes Musicales in Tijuana, which was inaugurated in 2012. See The Official OBC Website, www.cam-bc.org/obc, and "Inauguración del Centro de Artes Musicales de Tijuana", YouTube [video], uploaded December 13, 2012, www.youtube.com/watch?v=eXoDpNimhSc (Both accessed: November 18, 2019).

10. Born in 1978, Claire Chase grew up in the San Diego area and is now an international soloist and an influential arts entrepreneur. She was named "the most important flutist of our time" by the *New York Times*, and I would completely agree with that bold claim. See www.clairechase.net/ (Accessed: November 19, 2019).

11. The dance troupe was led by choreographer Yuriria Harris and the musicians of the project were René Castro, Álvaro Díaz, Guillermo Díaz, and I. We presented the project at a festival called Ensenada Danza para Todos at the Teatro de la Ciudad in April of 1992.

12. The piece was called *Andante* and was never premiered, but a few friends read a couple of passages from it so I could have a loose idea of what it sounded like.

13. *13 Microcomedias*, composed by Álvaro Díaz and scored for piccolo, viola, and piano. The premiere took place in a venue called El Lugar del Juglar, Tijuana, May 1993.

14. *The Split Trilogy* is integrated by three very simple text scores written a bit under the influence of Pauline Oliveros' work: *Split (Journey)* (2011), for split toy piano (two players); *Split (Realm)* (2012), for solo drummer; and *Split (Being)* (2012), for any wind instrument (and audience).

15. Wilfrido Terrazas, *Tótem III: Estoy en el centro* (2019), for trumpet and contrabass. Unpublished score, p. 2.

16. Full personnel: Cal Tjader, vibes; Mark Levine, piano and Fender Rhodes; Roger Glenn, flute and percussion; Vince Lateano, drums and percussion; Rob Fisher, bass; Poncho Sánchez, congas and percussion. The original album was released as an LP in 1980 by Concord Records. Back then I had the album in cassette format, which I must have acquired in 1990 or 1991. A few years ago, I bought the CD reissue. See Cal Tjader, *La onda va bien*. [CD] Concord Records, 1980, CCD-4113.

17. Acronym for the Association for the Advancement of Creative Musicians, founded in Chicago in 1965 by Muhal Richard Abrams and others. See George E. Lewis, *A Power Stronger Than Itself: The AACM and American Experimental Music* (Chicago & London: University of Chicago Press, 2008).

18. Terrazas, *Tótem III: Estoy en el centro*, op. cit. Emphasis in the original. In a more recent piece [*Hexagram 57*], the performer is given the choice to take materials from the three growth modules in the score and freely combine them, thus making the structure even more flexible than in prior pieces. See Wilfrido Terrazas, [*Hexagram 57*] (2018), for solo prepared flute. Unpublished score, p. 2.

19. The *Torres* cycle is a group of works that celebrate the Cardinal Points. It is integrated by *Torre del Sur* (2014), for any number of string players; *Torre del Este* (2016–17), for any number of percussionists; *Torre del Norte* (2018), for any number of brass players; *Tótem I, Camino sobre la tierra* (2019), for oboe and percussion; *Tótem II, Miro hacia el cielo* (2019), for any number of piccolo players; *Tótem III, Estoy en el centro* (2019), for trumpet and contrabass; and *Torre del Oeste* (planned for 2020), for woodwinds.

20. Founded in 2016, the Sea Quintet features José Solares on saxophone, Iván Trujillo on trumpet, Edwin Montes on guitar, José Luis Rodríguez on bass, Abraham Lizardo on drums, and myself on flute and whistles. The group started out first as a quartet, then became a quintet and is now a sextet, but keeps the same name as an homage to Henry Threadgill's *Sextett*, which used to have seven members.

Our debut album, *Pirate Songs*, featured two of my tunes, "Song for Peter" (2014) and "Song for Aimée" (2016), plus compositions by the other members of the band. See Wilfrido Terrazas, Sea Quintet. *Pirate Songs*. [CD] Ápice, 2018, AP003.

21. I am the first Mexican citizen ever to be hired as a full-time faculty member at UCSD's Department of Music. It is also exciting to realize that currently we have five Mexican students enrolled in our graduate program, which I believe is the highest number in the history of the Department. They are flutist Teresa Díaz de Cossio, vocalists Mariana Flores Bucio and Miguel Zazueta, and composers Andrés Gutiérrez and Jacques Zafra.

Recordings

Tjader, Cal. *La onda va bien*. [CD] Concord Records, 1980, CCD-4113.
Wilfrido Terrazas Sea Quintet. *Pirate Songs*. [CD] Ápice, 2018, AP003.

Unpublished Scores by Wilfrido Terrazas

Ariete (2006–07), for flute, clarinet in B flat, amplified guitar and percussion (9')
Heterofonía Ia (para G.L.) (2007), improvisation proposal for a flutist and electro-acoustic media (6')
Into White Tunnels of Wind (2007), for any wind instrument and AM/FM radio receiver (7')
Ítaca, viaje para un flautista (2012), nine pieces for solo flute (35')
Luna de estambre (2019), for two improvising soloists and open ensemble (variable duration)
Mosquito War Grooves (2009), for a mixed ensemble of improvising musicians (6')
Retrato de Walter Lärmer (2011–12), for a mixed ensemble of improvising musicians (variable duration)
Split (Being) (2012), for any wind instrument (variable duration)
Split (Journey) (2011), for split toy piano (two players, variable duration)
Split (Realm) (2012), for solo drummer (variable duration)
A String Set (2008–09), four pieces for any bowed string instrument (12')
Torre del Este (2016–17), for percussion (any number of players, variable duration)
Torre del Norte (2018), for any number of brass players (variable duration)
Torre del Sur (2014), five bowed string parts to be played in any combination (variable duration)
Tótem I, Camino sobre la tierra (2019), for oboe and percussion (variable duration)
Tótem II, Miro hacia el cielo (2019), for any number of piccolo players (variable duration)
Tótem III, Estoy en el centro (2019), for trumpet and contrabass (variable duration)
Varesiana (2006), improvisation proposal for three or more musicians (variable duration)

Websites

Centro Cultural Tijuana. www.cecut.gob.mx/acerca.php (Accessed: November 17, 2019).

Claire Chase, Flutist. www.clairechase.net/ (Accessed: November 19, 2019).

"Inauguración del Centro de Artes Musicales de Tijuana". YouTube video, uploaded December 13, 2012. www.youtube.com/watch?v=eXoDpNimhSc (Accessed: November 18, 2019).

Orquesta de Baja California. www.cam-bc.org/obc (Accessed: November 18, 2019).

San Diego Youth Symphony. https://sdys.org/about/ (Accessed: November 17, 2019).

Universidad Autónoma de Baja California, Facultad de Artes, Ensenada. http://artes. ens.uabc.mx/index.php (Accessed: November 18, 2019).

4 P/T

Ensenada and Experimentalist Musical Practice: Narrations in Place and Time

Teresa Díaz de Cossio and Paul N. Roth

Ensenada, a (Very) Brief Overview

The land on which Ensenada exists today—beside a bay, on Mexico's far west Pacific peninsular coast—is, firstly, home to Kumeyaay Native Americans. European missionaries (Jesuits, then Dominicans) were active in the region from the 16th century until 1845, when Mexico's new secular constitution following its war of independence from Spain reclaimed religious property for the state.[1] As a township, Ensenada was established in 1882 and a year later the Mexican Law of Colonization permitted foreigners to acquire large extensions of territory for development.[2] Since then, Ensenada has grown on particularly international terms. Early 19th-century reports note weekly bilingual newspapers, various expatriate business ventures (an Italian spaghetti factory, an American candle company, Russian and Spanish wineries,[3] Jewish banking enterprises)[4] as well as port receipts from Germany, China, Holland, France, India, England, Turkey, and the US.[5] In 1930, during US Prohibition, the Hotel Riviera del Pacífico opened on Ensenada's harbor, bringing glamour and cosmopolitanism to town and instilling a sense of sophistication that in many ways remains today.[6] These years also saw the paving of a road to Tijuana, further connecting Ensenada to its northern neighbors. A steady flow of arriving Mexican migrant workers doubled during World War II as the country installed a large military base on its outskirts. Ensenada's seafood canneries also flourished in this period (one can still smell these, traveling between El Sauzal and Ensenada proper). The later 20th century witnessed further expansion: manufacturing, science research centers, shipping, fishing, and mining activities advanced with concomitant population increases, accompanied by periods of both rapid economic growth and crisis.[7]

Today the city is home to roughly 300,000 inhabitants[8] with a high-volume port (the only deep-water port on the peninsula) and a broadening tourism sector of almost-daily cruise ship visits, eclectic international dining, drinking, and other consumptive fare, an increasingly-recognized wine region in nearby Valle de Guadalupe, plus the taquerías, panaderías, regional grocers, and music bars which give much of Mexico undeniable distinction. For a final anecdote, celebrated Baja California-based poet Gabriel Trujillo Muñoz characterizes Ensenada as a "classical, Europe-influenced, sophisticated town, an alternative to the vulgar Tijuana, the ultimate city-of-passing".[9] And with this we should keep in mind: Ensenada is at once isolated from central Mexico (Mexico City is almost 3,000 km away), easily accessible to San Diego (130 km), yet still a comfortable distance (100 km) from Tijuana's more troubling notorieties. As such, it maintains its tourist-friendly "destination" allure for nationals and foreigners alike.

Our Dialogue

P: So Teresa, I suppose we should contextualize the whole Ensenadensan scene a bit, which anyway has such a fascinating history.

T: Right. And we can probably start with Ernesto Rosas [*b. Ensenada, 1951*].

P: Yeah. He's definitely the "father" of the scene, kind of a mythical figure in Ensenada.

T: And I guess this really begins with Ernesto's father, Susano Rosas Zúñiga [*b. Mulegé, 1906–88*]. He was raised in Baja California but as a teenager his family moved to Los Angeles, running away from the government of Porfirio Díaz. There Susano studied harmony with Arnold Schoenberg after Schoenberg retired from UCLA, and he would refer to Schoenberg as the great harmonist (he often quoted Schoenberg's "dissonances do not exist, they are more advanced consonances"). At the time, Susano worked as conductor of a rumba orchestra and as one of the first cartoonists for Walt Disney, doing backgrounds for *Snow White*. Having a good socioeconomic status he married a Lebanese woman, but their relationship ended badly. Susano and his siblings eventually moved from Los Angeles to Ensenada, a period when they were giving land for free, to get Baja California more populated and avoid external invasion. There he had a rough start, but eventually Susano became a piano teacher and technician. That's how he met his second wife and mother of his five kids, María del Refugio Montoya, who everyone called "Doña Cuquita". And Susano was Ernesto's first piano teacher, his first main influence.

P: So, from early on an Ensenada-Los Angeles musical connection was established. And Susano sets the stage for Ernesto's musical development, getting him interested in modern classical music.

T: Yes. And Ernesto eventually gets into jazz as well. He told us the radio was a big influence for this, with broadcasts coming from the US, jazz and rock 'n' roll. Of course in Ensenada, they didn't have any coverage from Mexico City because it was too far away, so radio was dominated by American broadcasts.

P: And aside from the radio, he's going up regularly to Tower Records in San Diego for LP's in his youth. I liked his strategy: he'd take a pile of ten, divide them in half to five, cut that down to three, then two, and finally end up with the only one he had money for. There was also one record shop in Ensenada, with classical music and a bit of jazz.

T: Yeah. And there, he would hide his favorite records at the back of the shelves if he didn't have money to buy them at the time [*laughs*]. He was also coming to the US often for concerts when he was young. There was a museum in La Jolla, a contemporary art museum, and they were having regular events with contemporary music, for example.

P: So, growing up, he's into contemporary classical music from his father, he's into jazz, he's coming back and forth between San Diego and Los Angeles and Ensenada for musical things. But then, when he's ready for university, he moves to Mexico City to study Western classical composition at the Conservatorio Nacional, correct?[10]

T: Yes. Well, that's what he was trying to do! But when he arrived in Mexico City the enrollment dates had already passed (this was 1976, before on-line enrollment!). So instead Ernesto found Aurelio León-Ptanick, a former student of Susano. Aurelio had already graduated from the conservatory and studied for a PhD in Germany. As a teacher at the conservatory, Aurelio recommended Ernesto to study composition with Julio Estrada [*b. 1943*] and piano with Velia Nieto [*1943–2008: Nieto and Estrada were married*].[11] Later, Ernesto enrolled at the Escuela Nacional de Música at UNAM,[12] studying piano with Velia and composition with Mario Lavista [*b. 1943*].[13]

P: And, just for clarity, Mario Lavista and Julio Estrada were two of the more important contemporary music Mexican composers at the time, right?

T: Correct. But they had very different aesthetics. Julio Estrada was more avant-garde. Mario Lavista was following other aesthetics, a bit more conservative. In particular Ernesto and Julio Estrada became close friends, even though Ernesto never officially studied with him.

P: And we should note the '70s was an interesting period in Mexico City: rock 'n' roll had fully arrived but was censured by the government. Lots of leftist student protests were happening. The universities were debating Marxism and class struggles. The Mexican hippy movement was in full swing [*los jipitecas*].[14] It seems there was lots of energy.

T: Yes. And there's something else here too: Ernesto told me it was an interesting environment with Mario Lavista and the university, because most of the students were kind of high-class. They had lots of money. And in the beginning, they saw Ernesto as, "Oh, you just come from Ensenada", and when they would have parties or go out, they would never invite him.

P: Hmm. Well I know it was a time when Mexico's middle and upper-middle classes were growing.[15] I didn't realize Ensenada was seen as a rural, backwards place in their mind though. That's interesting.

T: I thought so too. But at the same time, being from Baja California, Mario Lavista suggested Ernesto go to University of California at San Diego (UCSD).[16] At the time, Ernesto knew of the school, because before moving to Mexico City he used to visit the library with his brother and go to concerts.

P: Yeah, so UCSD already had a respected reputation within these global contemporary music scenes. And Ernesto follows Lavista's advice, right? He comes back to Baja California, applies to UCSD. He gets in, but in the end he can't afford to go, and he's totally depressed. So he starts playing jazz in bars in Ensenada, the first musician to initiate that according to him. Before it was only rock and música tropical.[17]

T: Yes, he's playing in bars at night, he's also teaching music in a kindergarten in the day. Actually that's how he meets his wife, who was also a kindergarten teacher. They get married, they have a son, Carlos, and eventually Ernesto feels a responsibility to provide his son with a quality music education, so he starts working with a music school that had just recently begun, the Centro de Estudios Musicales (CEM).[18]

P: And this is really important, right? Because CEM, which is essentially a youth orchestra with some preparatory classes—and the only music program for young kids at the time—would eventually be taken under the wing of the local university (UABC) and would mentor many developing students.[19] I guess we should also mention the Orquesta de Baja California (OBC)?

T: Yes, and the Russians![20]

P: The Russians, of course! And Eduardo García Barrios.

T: Yes. He's a conductor, from Mexico City. He went to study in Moscow for some time, and then moves to Ensenada. In the process he invites these seven classically trained, very talented Russian musicians he met in Moscow back to Baja California, just after the collapse of the Soviet Union. They help start the OBC, an orchestra performing more-traditional Western classical repertoire, and they also teach at CEM.

P: And we were told they kind of upped the ante in terms of instrumental virtuosity and technique, bringing this into their teaching as well. I've heard funny stories of terrified students around this time, getting yelled at in Russian if they didn't practice enough!

T: Oh yeah [*laughs*]. And while this is going on, Ernesto also starts inviting adventurous musicians—many of them from the US—to come and do workshops and concerts for CEM and sometimes with the Orquesta de Baja California.

P: Right. And this is funny: he told us that, to make this work, with the guests—because there was hardly ever any money—he would drive to LA to, for example, pick up Terry Riley and bring him back down to Ensenada. And when Ernesto wanted the Arditti Quartet but couldn't afford their fee, he promised them lobster every day, which Puerto Nuevo had a reputation for.[21]

T: Oh right! [*laughs*] There was also Daniel Catán who came, who taught with Mario Lavista. Ernesto also studied composition with him in Mexico City. And Ernesto brought Julio Estrada a few times as well, to do workshops with the youth orchestra [*CEM*].

P: And I feel that's important, because it sets the foundation for visiting artists and the workshop emphasis, which becomes very central as we move forward with the history of the scene.

T: And it's important also that Ernesto helps CEM expand into a music bachelor's degree, finally created at UABC in 2003. Reflecting on this, I guess his first son Carlos must have been a driving force for all this, right? Because it happens when Carlos was about to finish high school. And I'm also thinking, Ernesto must have learned this from his mother! Ernesto's younger brother was born with a developmental disability, and at the time there weren't any schools in Ensenada to accommodate him. So Doña Cuquita decided to found the first school in the city for kids with special needs.

P: That's a great observation. So he was really being a caring father [*laughs*]. And also, in the process, setting a strong foundation for all this: he's a big influence in the development of CEM, he's bringing exciting musicians from the US, helps solidify the music degree in the university, he's introducing all these different musical styles and aesthetics, he also starts a jazz festival which we can talk more about. And obviously, if Ensenada weren't so close to major urban centers in the United States, none of this would be possible.[22]

T: Yeah, because flying these musicians further down into Mexico would be much more expensive than just driving them from the border.

P: Right, and even for a place like Mexicali, it doesn't have a large US city to easily dialogue with, like Ensenada and Tijuana do with San Diego and LA.[23] So, what comes next?

T: Well, I thought we could move to the next generations, perhaps Wilfrido Terrazas [*flute, b. Camargo, 1974*] and Álvaro G. Díaz Rodríguez [*oboe, b. Ensenada, 1973*]?[24]

P: Sure, because Willy and Álvaro were kind of Ernesto's top student pro-teges. They come up through CEM, they also told us about going to Ernesto's house when they were young, checking out his record collection and talking music. I know that's where Willy was first introduced to Webern, Varèse, Ligeti, Xenakis, Stockhausen, Cage, as well as Ornette Coleman, the AACM and other avant-garde jazz groups, for example.

T: Yeah, and they follow a similar pattern as Ernesto. First, Ernesto would drive them all together in his van up to San Diego for music. Then, when they were older and Álvaro had a car, he and Willy would go on their own. They'd make hard copies of lots of scores at the UCSD library, with piles and piles of music that they would bring back. They were also taking lessons on their instruments [*in San Diego*].

P: Willy told me stories of going by bus too, making a whole day out of it: Ensenada to the border, to UCSD, to downtown for his teacher and record shops, and back, long trip! But then they eventually both migrate away. Willy goes to Morelia, to El Conservatorio de las Rosas, and Álvaro goes to UNAM, in Mexico City.

T: Right, Álvaro goes to study performance and starts attending the composition class of Julio Estrada, probably from Ernesto's influence. This was a difficult time to be a student at UNAM, because there were continuous protests and all the activities related to the university stopped for over a year [*in 1999*]. As a consequence, Álvaro lost his job doing archive work at the Instituto de Investigaciones Estéticas, an affiliated institution. So he comes back to Baja California to continue his education, finishing his bachelor's degree in History at UABC, a master's degree at UABC in Pedagogy, and then his PhD in Buenos Aires.

P: And Willy, I know he comes back to Ensenada after las Rosas, but a few years later moves to Mexico City and starts getting more and more into improvisation.[25] In 2006, for example, he helps found the free improvisation group Generación Espontánea, and that seems to have been an important experience for him.[26] He told me he never wanted to be in Mexico City, by the way. He moved there with his then-wife. But anyway, he stays for 14 years. And meanwhile, he's traveling back to Ensenada and begins these improvisation workshops, which were the first of their kind there, and turn out to be hugely important moving forward, right?

T: Yes, and at this point I feel we should move to Iván Trujillo [*trumpet, b. Ensenada, 1980*]. He studied with Ernesto's brother Bebo when he was young, who also taught at CEM. Then later he graduates from UABC in Ensenada, and he and Willy would start working together on various projects as Iván gets older.[27]

P: And Iván has an interesting story. He lived in LA and NYC for a while, getting intimidated at jam sessions and playing in salsa bands to make ends meet. He also moves briefly to Barcelona pursuing music. But he eventually comes back to Ensenada, somewhat reluctantly, to monitor his Dad's health, and at this point [*in 2013*] he establishes "La Covacha", right?

T: Right. La Covacha was a collective venue in downtown Ensenada he starts with Julia Chávez Remigio [*b. Ensenada, 1982*]—she was Iván's partner at the time—and visual artist Esther Gámez [*b. Hermosillo, 1979*]. They were doing original music, art exhibitions, and other noncommercial things. Esther was giving art classes, they had other types of classes as well.

P: And La Covacha is the first venue for independent music and art activities in Ensenada. But it closes after a while. I guess there wasn't enough interest to keep it going, and Iván told me it was difficult getting people to pay door fees for musicians. Meanwhile though, Iván also starts La Semana Internacional de Improvisación.[28] And I suppose this is the important connection with Willy and the improv workshops, because Iván continues this format, and the workshops become an important pillar for these festivals.

T: Yes. And I can say Willy's workshops really empowered many new generations of musicians. Plus, the events continued bringing great artists from San Diego, Los Angeles, and Mexico City: Carmina Escobar [*voice, LA*] came, Stephanie Richards [*trumpet, San Diego*], Vinny Golia [*winds, LA*], Dario Bernal [*percussion, Mexico City*], Nathan Hubbard [*drums, San Diego*], Stevart Liebig [*bass, LA*]. And they all offer workshops free and open to students, with concerts in the evening.

P: And through these many workshops and festivals with visiting artists, all these other successive generations of younger musicians become interested in improvisation and experimentalist music.

T: Exactly! And of course there are students even younger, who continue to come up through the university music program, and gradually get into new music and improvisation through Álvaro's contemporary music course, and the combinations of festivals and workshops going on in the year.[29]

P: And you more or less lived through all this, right? Can you share a little about your own experience?

T: Yes of course! Where shall we start?

P: Well, I know you attended CEM in your high school years, and then went on to study music at university. Was it there, at UABC, where you got introduced to all these experimentalist musical activities?

T: I definitely became curious through some of the festivals before university, I remember that for sure. And then, during my bachelor's, we had

Álvaro's Ensemble de Música Contemporanea, and I started performing contemporary works. We'd play some Stockhausen, Cage, Berio, and Dallapicola, for example.

P: And I guess we should note that Álvaro is a bit of a character, I imagine especially as a teacher. In his music history class, for example, he had students watch Wagner's entire *Ring* cycle, right?

T: Yes it was a complete day, starting early in the morning and ending at 1 or 2 am!

P: That's a bit nuts [*laughs*]. And he's also a strong believer in new music for all levels of musicianship. He's had pushback over the years at UABC for his contemporary music ensemble, but as he joked to me, "Plenty of people play Beethoven poorly, so why worry about playing Stockhausen poorly too?"

T: That sounds about right [*laughs*].

P: And how about after your bachelor's?

T: Well, as I told you before, everyone in my generation was trained to be classical, plus we had the Russian influence with a very technical and precise orchestral training. Even Ernesto, he was always talking about orchestras and orchestral jobs. That was kind of the figure of success. We'd had other colleagues from earlier generations, traditional players, who finished at UABC and then continued their studies at San Diego State University [*SDSU*], to keep pursuing an orchestral training. I was interested in that, and honestly I didn't know much about other schools beyond San Diego, I didn't have many friends doing similar things back in those days. The thing is in Ensenada you grow up there, and you're so isolated from the rest of Mexico. You basically have no idea of other programs in the country and things like that. And I remember I spoke to Willy, back then I thought I wanted to have an orchestral career, and he said "just go to the States". So I applied to SDSU and got accepted, but I didn't get the money to go and I declined the offer, and I really didn't know what I was going to do. I was teaching a bit, to kids, flute lessons at CEM after I graduated, but I hadn't figured out the rest.

P: But then something strange and noteworthy happens, right? I remember this [*laughs*].

T: Yes, this is a great story! Just after I graduated, there was a very rich family, in San Diego, who were moving to Beijing with their kids, and they wanted someone who could teach them Spanish and flute. So, they decided to call the OBC, and see if they'd recommend anyone. A few of us got a call about it, and to be honest, everybody thought it wasn't for real, because—no joke—they were offering to pay $1,000 a week, plus expenses![30]

P: Wow! That's a lot of money!

T: Yes, and that was 2009! So I called, I went up to do the interview in San Diego, and they accepted me right away. Two weeks later (August of 2009) I was flying to Beijing, and I worked with them for the next eight months. That was great, because I was also lucky to continue my studies with the flutist from the National Conservatory. Honestly, I felt behind. I knew I needed to catch up as a player. And that was something I think, it got ingrained in my brain by Ernesto, because he would always say, "The level outside Ensenada is so high, you need to practice more and more and more!" And so, that's why I continued to take lessons. It was a nice time though, I remember. I was living close to the Beijing National Center for the Performing Arts. The apartment was only one or two subway stations away, so I was able to go to concerts after work. The program was very traditional, but it was nice to hear such a professional orchestra. And I also saved lots of money. I bought a new flute with part of it. And when I came back, I decided to finally do the master's degree at SDSU, and I was able to pay for that too [*2011–13*].

P: What an amazing opportunity! And what happened then, after SDSU?

T: I returned to Ensenada and was doing different teaching jobs in the region, at UABC and a community program in Tijuana, and also studying with the associate principal from the LA Phil, still trying to follow a more traditional classical path. I was going there on the bus! [*laughs*] It was taking me the whole day there and back, which was a bit crazy. It was nice though: my teacher was hardly charging me, and the lessons were at Disney Hall (where the LA Philharmonic performs). After classes sometimes, if I didn't have to rush back, I could see the orchestra rehearse and that was sooo much fun. Because it's a great orchestra. And they were playing new works too. But honestly all this was very tiring, and the community programs in Tijuana didn't pay well at all. Sometimes they ran three or four months behind with paychecks. I was thinking to study again, and my old teacher at SDSU suggested I apply to SUNY Purchase, so I did, I got a scholarship and could work as well, so I decided to do that.

P: Ah that's right, we talked about this before. And that's when the new music direction really took off for you, correct?

T: Yes, Purchase ended up being great for this, for new music. It changed me. None of my flute teachers before had done anything with extended techniques and that, and here I could really get into it. And honestly, new music became more engaging for me once I started to actively play it, experimenting with extended techniques and all of that. Before, I'd never really had a chance to try. Which, I'm grateful for all the things my teachers taught me before, of course, but now I was getting a chance to do something different. And it was there at Purchase where I also started doing serious collaborations with composers, and that was so much fun. And the scene there is huge, in Purchase and NYC, and new music was a core part of our education. We had ensembles, we used to get assigned two or three new pieces every semester. And, with the job I had repairing flutes in Manhattan, I was close to everything, and I was going there twice per week, so it was easy for me after work to go to concerts. The NY Public Library had a free series of contemporary music concerts, and other times I would go touring to all the places where you could see events.

P: And so you eventually finished at Purchase in 2018. Did you already know about UCSD?

T: I'd realized I'd wanted to continue studying this kind of music for sure. And I found out Willy had just started teaching here. Álvaro told me while I was doing my DMA applications: "Willy's there at UCSD now, why don't you apply? It's free, you know". And I thought, "Well, sure I'll apply if it's free!" And yes, I was aware they had a good program.

P: And, I guess, meanwhile, you'd been away for a while, did you know all this exciting stuff with contemporary music and improvisation had been developing further in Ensenada?

T: I did, because my sisters were there, they were both doing their bachelor's at UABC.[31] And they would tell me they were taking improvisation workshops with Willy, and Rocío for example took a conduction/improvisation course with Stephanie Richards that she liked.[32] It was all very exciting for them I think.

P: And then your sisters went to study in the States too, after UABC? Is that kind of the goal, finishing the bachelor's at home in Ensenada and then looking to grad school in the US?

T: Well, there are more scholarships and funding, for one thing. We don't have so much of that in Mexico for graduate programs. And I guess the schools in the US have better reputations too.

P: And other big cities in Latin America—say, Buenos Aires or Rio—they aren't really on the map for you all in that context?

T: No, I guess not.

P: Well, shall we move on to the actual festival? What motivated you to organize it?

T: Sure. Basically, there weren't summer programs in the area—or in any other state close by—to which my students from the university were able to attend. I think it's important they get to work with other teachers and meet other musicians. When Stefanie Proulx [*co-organizer for the first Festival Música Nueva Ensenada*] decided to come, I asked her if she could teach them, and Willy was also on board. Accessibility was an important element from the beginning, plus the idea of bringing new music to kids and other people.

P: Right. And so, I'm curious how this festival is working locally, because it seems you have, for example, some of the free improvisation folks with Willy's band,[33] who work within jazz realms writing and playing their own music, and then also doing more popular musics, like cumbia or funk or Brazilian-influenced musics in some of the fancier wineries. And these are some of the same musicians who cross over into the new music activities as well, and vice-versa.

T: Yes, that's new for me. In Purchase, for example, we didn't really have any improvisation scene at all. And of course to my knowledge we didn't have anyone playing cumbia! We had the jazz department, they were doing their stuff, and we were doing new music. I mean, we would support one another between those two, but it was different scenarios. We were not collaborating in between. And when I would show friends things we were doing here [*in Ensenada*] with free improvisation, they would say "What's that!? That sounds so weird!"

P: So I guess my question would be then, in Ensenada, do you find these aesthetics more mixed, where there's more overlap between practitioners?

T: Yeah, and I think it's great. Also, we have to remember there aren't so many musicians doing these types of things in Ensenada: we need to be able to be flexible.

P: Totally. And I agree, it seems refreshing and super healthy not having such strict divides and hierarchies about who can do free improvisation, who can do new music, who does more popular-based musics. I suppose this ties clearly into issues of migration: you have musicians spending time in much larger urban settings with more people, more infrastructure, more institutions, and then bringing these ideas back to a much smaller environment, everybody gets wrapped up into everything. And how about the festival structure itself? There were four days of workshops and concerts throughout the city. I really enjoyed your venue selection in particular. Can we talk about that?

T: Of course! The first night we were at the university, the second was in the jail, the third in El Studio BC [*a private recording studio*], and the final in Bodegas de Santo Tomás, the old winery in downtown.

P: The jail sticks out right away! What was that about?

T: It's not a jail anymore [*laughs*]. Now it's a museum.[34] And it was funny because, I think, probably we did concerts there many years ago. They don't normally do concerts, they're a museum after all. We'd first planned to use the Riviera [*the Prohibition-era upscale hotel/casino; see our Ensenada overview*], but they needed some electrical work done so they canceled on us. We'll probably do the jail again because it worked so well, but we'd also like to do the Riviera next year because I think it's also nice.

P: And I guess, a larger question with all this—maybe it's obvious—why put these events in unusual concert spaces? I mean, the university is the university. But the others seem much less conventional.

T: Well, in the beginning we were planning to use the university for everything. But then, the people who work at the theatre were on vacation. And I was told, "You cannot bring them early, they will get so mad!" And I said ok, we need to find alternate spaces. But it kind of put us in a very good situation because, being outside of where we usually work, I think it attracts more public.

P: Ahhh! See I thought the idea all along was to have unusual venues!

T: Not in the beginning. But then I was thinking, "This could actually work very well". And the spaces were very generous. We only had to pay small fees to use them, just for the maintenance, some permits and stuff like that. It was a bit of a sponsorship.

P: And, well, sometimes with new music and the spaces it happens in, it's definitely up there in the hierarchy of things. It's not necessarily street Banda music, it's not Hussong's.[35]

T: I think it can be but the idea with this festival was to not put this music in that scenario.

P: Do you think the audiences felt that, with the ways these venues framed things differently?

T: By speaking to some of the audience members, I got a sense, for many of them it was their first time going to new music events. So, it was weird for them to hear it, it's so so different from what they're used to listening to. But I think the spaces made things more comfortable.

P: It's certainly less stuffy and more accessible, not being in the concert hall.

T: Yeah. Plus the idea of not having chairs, so we were able to move freely, for example [*at El Studio BC and Bodegas de Santo Tomás*]. But it was also budget [*laughs*]. Renting chairs was expensive! And we didn't have money. So we had to use, as Willy says, "every disadvantage as an advantage".

P: Totally! I'm thinking about that last concert, especially during the Pauline Oliveros piece,[36] where all these musicians were doing actions, and then audience members were walking around and looking over musician's shoulders at music stands, trying to figure out what was going on: I felt that was so open and liberating. I mean, new music can have a stubborn elitist sensibility. And you're getting away from that.

T: Yes, absolutely. It makes it more accessible, in every sense. That's why we emphasized kids enrolling, we didn't put any restrictions on whether you had experience or not doing music, you were able to join. Everyone could do the accompanying workshops for free, regardless of musical background.

P: Agreed, having free and open workshops with all these talented guest clinicians and performers—I know you advertised as well to some of the community music programs for less privileged kids—that seems really important and impactful for the whole festival. I feel too that, say, in a place like Bodegas de Santo Tomás, it's also the site of the annual Verbena.[37] Do you feel it connects with a more-general popular imagination, as a very traditional Ensenada activity? In the sense that people know this as a vernacular space, part of everyday culture as long as most folks can remember?

T: Probably, and that's something that, after I realized we weren't going to have the theatre, I was looking for spaces that were accessible in every sense, right? Where the public didn't have to pay, that were easy to get to, spaces they knew, and particularly not concert halls, so we could explore that option as well, and spaces that might provide a different sense for the music.

P: Yeah. And I guess that's part of Ensenada: it's quite small and you have to negotiate all these things because of much different infrastructures and options. I feel that's what makes it so special and unique, dealing with uncertainties and creative constraints. Kind of like finding your own way.

T: Right. And I really like working in Ensenada: you're able to create because you're doing new stuff, you're able to put some parameters of what you want to do. And in this case, I felt: well, we still have a lot of work to do, but in a way I feel we kind of achieved this goal of making new music accessible to all. And that's the point, that new music isn't something you need to study for so many years to get to. Or, I don't know, there are many ideas in this music that I don't think are necessarily true. For a time, I didn't feel prepared to do new music, because I had this idea that in order to do it you need to be so so good on your instrument, the top level as a player. Plus I didn't have the teachers, as we spoke before. I'll say, in my education, I got this general sense that new music was so hard. But now I don't think so. Because one of the first things you do on flute is make multiphonics for example, because you cannot get just one note [*laughs*]. And you do lots of great air tones. Now I have my young students improvise right away and they do amazing things! So, I don't think it's a necessarily high level of stuff.

P: Yeah, it reminds of that 9-year-old boy, who did the percussion duet during the concert at Bodegas de Santo Tomás with Miguel A. Cuevas, his percussion instructor, which was such a wonderful moment!

T: That boy invented that piece! And I think that was also a larger result, because all the kids were going to Willy's improv classes during the festival, then Amy's improv sessions with puppetry, and then they were working with their own individual instrument teachers.[38]

P: So again, the workshop element is really vital. I wonder, did you encounter festivals that also had a workshop element in NYC?

T: Not really. But in fact I didn't go to many festivals there. Do you have experience with this?

P: I rarely see the workshop/festival combination. It seems people don't have the energy. Or artists feel they're too important to come down and engage with students who might have no experience. I think it can be a hierarchy thing.

T: That's a good point.

P: And speaking of hierarchies, you programmed one evening that was only Mexican young composers, which I feel touches on lots of interesting issues in this music.

T: Yeah, it was pretty much people less than 40, mostly whom we knew, from Baja California.

P: "Young!"

T: Young! Yup, I want to think [*laughs*].

P: And so, obviously, that seems totally appropriate. I imagine it'd seem silly bringing only American or French, or whoever else "Western" composers and present them in Ensenada. Does that help give everyone a more local sense of place and significance?

T: Sure of course. We also had a few people from other states in Mexico and one of them was a composer, Cynthia Beatriz Martínez Lira. She came from Guadalajara, we performed her piece as well.

P: And, so, I know it's obvious, but why is that important for you, featuring these composers?

T: Because they just don't get the space and exposure. And I feel their work is so valuable. And I feel that for us as performers it's important to play their work and keep it alive.

P: And, say, when you were at Purchase, were you playing Mexican composers?

T: We didn't play them at all, and I definitely felt frustration with that! I remember once I brought a Mario Lavista piece in and no one knew who Lavista was. And, for me, he was one of the big names in Mexico! And, I was just surprised. But then, instead of feeling frustrated, I thought this was our job to bring those composers out. Old generations and new generations as well.

P: So in fact you're doing a bit of an activist-repertoire.

T: I guess so! And for the future—this year it didn't work so well [*laughs*]— but one of the things I'd like to try to accomplish is to take these concert programs elsewhere. So, we'll have the festival, but then if we can present those concerts, like here too [*in San Diego*], as well as other parts of Mexico. It will definitely require much more budget, which is always hard, but I think it's important we promote the work of our own composers.

P: Of course. And I feel that, in these contemporary music spheres, it's so easy to say "the European and American composers and schools and canons", while these other geographic places get completely left out. If folks like you don't do it, they might never get out there at all.

T: Exactly. And I feel one of the reasons is that, in Ensenada, there's no composition school or program either. There's no infrastructure to help promote and support it that way. In Mexico City, for example, there are many festivals and programs for new music. I was just there researching more about them. Something I learned as well which is important, doing some interviews, is that whenever someone gets a grant from the government, they need to do something for the community. So, as I was talking to young artists, they would say, "Oh yeah, I started learning about this technique or this way of composition when I went to those courses that were taught by people who had grants from the government".

P: Ah ok, because they offer a workshop course, something like that? For individual grants?

T: Yes, individual grants for musicians. And then they have to offer something free for the community. And I feel this tends to happen in Mexico City, but not so much in Baja California. The grants are open to all Mexicans, but not so many artists in our region receive them. Of course, there are many fewer musicians in Baja California than in, say, Mexico City. But I'd be curious to know where those grants are going in numbers. I'll look into that.[39]

P: That's a good point. And speaking of numbers, if we go back to your festival and talk about gender representation, because it's come up before: when you program the festival, are you also trying to make sure and have a balance of women participants? Is that something you consider?

T: Umm . . . yes. Well, it's double-sided. You want to include women because, not necessarily because they are only women. But, for example, this concert of young Mexican composers: there were two women composers and six men.

P: I suppose if you had more money, would you target women composers from other parts of the country, with the resources to bring them?

T: I think we shall be mindful. But, after doing some research, I think it's also important not just that they're women, but what they can bring to the community. But at least this time we had women composers on each of the four events.[40]

P: And maybe we can just talk about the numbers and gender representation of the invited guests clinicians and artists, and where they all come from to make this happen?

T: Sure. Well, women, we had many [*laughs*]! They were here [*at UCSD*], and they offered. Amy Cimini [*violist*] came, Rebecca Lloyd-Jones [*percussion*] and Alexandria Smith [*recording techniques*] as well. Stefanie Proulx [*flute and festival co-founder*] and Martha Rolón [*clarinet*] came from New York. Carmina Escobar [*LA, voice*] was coming but she couldn't last minute, so Miguel Zazueta filled in. Then there was Armando de la Torre with the puppets, also Elijah Rubottom and Walter Lawrance Sutin. Kevin Schwenkler [*piano*] came. And Willy of course.[41]

P: And I guess it's important to note that people offered their time out of goodwill, there wasn't compensation. It reminds me of Ernesto's story, sending a van (driven by Willy and Álvaro!) to LA from Ensenada to pick up the Arditti Quartet, and promising them abundant lobster as compensation. There's definitely an energy to these things, doing them on shoe-string budgets with people willing to donate time and energy. I feel that's rather special, versus events that are already well-funded. People seem to check out a bit, to have a different perspective of engagement and expectation.

T: Yes absolutely.

P: And on this topic, can we talk about funding real quick? Because I know that's crucial to all this too, and always a juggling act and struggle. You had some university support for the festival, at least with equipment, correct?

T: We had a little. They paid for some flights, for Ignacio Baca Lobera [*Mexico City–based composer*] and José Manuel Alcántara [*Mexico City–based guitarist*], and hotels for them as well. But I feel like these funding things are very different in the US and Mexico.

P: Tell me a little more about that, I'm curious.

T: Well, in the US you have plenty of private sponsors. There is something weird in Mexico, that when you talk to people about private sponsorship, it doesn't happen. During the festival, for example, I was trying like crazy to get money from private donors. What I got was helpful, like Javi from Boules: he donated one lunch for the entire group of teachers, and the bakery donated bread, and stuff like that.[42] But money coming from people, it was very difficult, there wasn't so much.

P: And I'm just thinking in the US, there are wealthy people and there are less wealthy people. Obviously these regions have very different economic realities. But, there are also wealthy people in Ensenada.

T: Yes, like all the people from the winery! They have plenty of money. I mean, you can give 100 pesos, right? That's not much. But I feel it's a different sense. In Mexico, for that stuff, we're so used to the government supporting everything.

P: You mean for art and culture?

T: Yes. Well now, we don't have much money. The government used to have special scholarships to do festivals and things like that. These days it's very hard.

P: And I guess one reason is the US has its degrees of corruption, but there are certainly degrees of corruption in Mexico that affect government funding.

T: Yes, we do have our troubles with that.

P: But you think funding has really dried up the past few years?

T: It seems that way. Even my mom, who works in science for the university system, is having harder times. And anyway, this time, for the festival, I will say 80% of our funding came from private donors here in the States!

P: Right, I noticed that you had a GoFundMe campaign, and lots of donations came from folks in and around San Diego, which certainly is nice to see that support! I also wonder, maybe tied to possible government funding, as you continue to program events like the New Music Festival: do you feel any importance to include traditional music aspects, looking at composers who work with more traditional styles, for example. Does that register for you?

T: I am thinking about it yes. And it's something that, as I'm working with the festival, what aim to give, if we could do a year of a particular style, or trying to focus on a particular aesthetic. But the side of cultural appropriation is always coming back to me. The thing is, not to just take those musics. We need to respect them. But I also feel it's important to honor them. I haven't come to the solution of how to do this work.

P: I can see how that's difficult. I mean, I feel that, with activities tied to the university, it automatically has a certain hierarchy through its cultural capital, as a particular platform for getting things out in certain ways. So then I wonder how it might also serve as platform for more traditional musics, which are also important of course, to have exposure at a similar level. And maybe there are instances where there might be new things going on within spheres of traditional music aesthetics. I'm not so sure how much that happens.

T: Well, I don't think so much. But there are spaces for that. Do you know the Festival Nativa, in spring in Ensenada?[43] It's an initiative created by the government to have all those traditions in place. They do live performances, people from different indigenous communities come and present their works, both crafts and music.

P: I didn't know that. I guess a fusion with different musics is difficult, and I suppose that's what you're worried about, that sort of appropriation, I can understand that.

T: Right. But in general, for the festival, I am trying to be careful of presenting a big range of aesthetics.

P: You want that?

T: Yes! Because I feel new music, experimenting with these sounds and directions, can incorporate so many different things and be meaningful for so many different people.

P: Agreed! Well, Mauricio might be upset with us if we go much longer. Shall we stop here?

T: Yes, thanks for the space and let's continue the conversation another day!

P/T: Postscript

Reflecting on our preceding dialogue, we feel we can offer a few parting thoughts towards which this material gestures. We hope, for one, we've illuminated the ways Ensenada's particular geography and history (its international beginnings as township; its sophisticated sensibility; its seclusion from central Mexico yet proximity to—and interaction with—San Diego and Los Angeles) provide possibilities and equilibriums for such experimentalist musical practices to emerge and grow. Here, we find UABC's institutional support, with targeted help from Rosas and Díaz alongside frequent collaborations with Terrazas and Trujillo, particularly meaningful for the scene's continued development.

The dialogue also details some of the ways musical thinking migrates around the world. In this particular instance, a mostly European-derived collection of practices (experimental music, improvised music, new music, etc.) are enacted under local circumstances by local (and regional) practitioners, with locally inflected aesthetics framed by their particular place and time. This becomes enriched further through travels of certain individuals to larger urban centers (national or international) and back again, bringing ideas, sensibilities, and so forth. These are then mobilized through, and respond to, their provincial environment.

Lastly, we acknowledge we've yet to provide any adequate definition of "experimentalist". For better or worse, we'll leave it at that (although we make a point to broaden typical boundaries of the term in endnote 42). We do hope, however, that the 2nd Festival de Música Nueva Ensenada shows ways contemporary music formats might evade some of the high-art elitisms they generally inhabit. We feel the strategies and approaches presented here—affordability, workshops requiring no prior musical experience, emphasis on local practitioners, creative selection of venues, etc.—open doors for larger publics to experiment with unusual, less-conventional, perhaps challenging sounds, forms, and ways of thinking. This can be as fun, profound, and curious as it is accessible and, as a result—as Díaz de Cossio says—"meaningful for so many different people".

Thanks to our interlocutors who generously donated their time throughout 2019: Julio Estrada, Ernesto Rosas, Álvaro Díaz, Wilfrido Terrazas, Boris Glouzman, Pavel Getman, David Martínez, Marilu Salinas, Gabriel Trujillo Muñoz, Iván Trujillo, Adnán Márquez Borbón, Esther Gámez, Edwin Montes Roldán, Matt Lamkin, José Luis Rodríguez, Dylan Brown, Kathia Rudametkin, Lesly Sandoval, José Solares, and Katherine Hernández.

Notes

1. Bonifaz de Novelo (1984), 8.
2. See Nordhoff (1888), p. 87.
3. Many of these missions established wineries and wine production continues to define contemporary Ensenada. For decades Bodegas de Santo Tomás, for instance, ran a large wine production facility downtown, a site that continues to host an annual summer wine festival. Bodegas de Santo Tomás recently celebrated their 150th anniversary as one of California's (both Alta and Baja's) oldest wineries and figures into our dialogue later.
4. Stern (1973), p. 33.
5. Bonifaz de Novelo, *op. cit.*
6. Today the structure is called the Centro Social, Cívico, y Cultural de Ensenada.
7. See Walker (2013).
8. Population data comes from http://cuentame.inegi.org.mx/monografias/informa cion/bc/poblacion/ (Accessed: December 2019).
9. In conversation with Gabriel Trujillo Muñoz, Mexicali, October 2019.
10. The Conservatorio Nacional de Música in Mexico City began in 1866.
11. Julio Estrada, Mexican composer and musicologist, studied composition in Mexico with Julian Orbón and in Europe with Oliver Messiaen, Nadia Boulanger, Henri Pousseur, György Ligeti, Iannis Xenakis, and Karlheinz Stockhausen. His PhD dissertation is *Théorie de la composition: Discontinuum-continuum*, University of Strasbourg, 1994. He currently teaches at UNAM and is a researcher at the Instituto de Investigaciones Estéticas. Monika Fürst-Heidtmann, *Grove Music Online.* https://doi.org/10.1093/gmo/9781561592630.article.47996 (Accessed: January 9, 2020).
12. UNAM is the Universidad Nacional Autónoma de México, founded in its modern form in 1910.
13. Mario Lavista is a Mexican composer who studied composition with Carlos Chávez at the Conservatorio Nacional and then with Iannis Xenakis, Henri Pousseur, and Karlheinz Stockhausen while living in Europe (1967–69). Upon his return to Mexico, Lavista founded the improvisation group Quanta and the journal *Pauta*. He currently teaches composition at Mexico City's Conservatorio. Ricardo Miranda Pérez, *Grove Music Online.* https://doi.org/10.1093/gmo/9781561592630.article.45207 (Accessed: January 9, 2020).
14. See Zolov (1999).
15. Walker, *op. cit.*
16. University of California, San Diego.
17. Rosas performs mostly bebop and hard bop jazz styles. For more on "musica tropical", see Rivera (1998) and/or Wade (2000).

18. CEM was founded in 1987 by Felix Mora and Helena Rousillo.
19. The UABC (Universidad Autónoma de Baja California) is the national public university of the state of Baja California, with campuses in Ensenada, Tijuana, and Mexicali. It was founded in 1957. The university began administering CEM in 1988.
20. The OBC began in 1990 and the Russian musicians arrived a year later.
21. The Arditti Quartet is based in the UK but was touring southern California at the time. Puerto Nuevo is 60 km north of Ensenada and continues to maintain reputations for exceptional lobster.
22. Other visiting musicians from San Diego or Los Angeles invited by Rosas in this period include Anthony Davis, JD Panan, Bertrand Turetsky, Steve Schick, Stefano Scodanibbio, and Ed Harkins.
23. Mexicali (pop. 1,000,000), the current capital of Baja California, is 160 km east of Tijuana on the US–Mexico border. Calexico (pop. 40,000) is its northern US border neighbor.
24. Terrazas is currently Assistant Professor of Music at UCSD. Díaz is Professor Investigador in the Music Department at UABC Ensenada.
25. Terrazas notes Vinko Globokar, Michel Portal, the French Orchestre National du Jazz, and Derek Bailey as early improvisation influences.
26. Generación Espontánea would evolve into an octet with broad international influences. Percussionist Dario Bernal Villegas, for instance, studied in London, notably with UK improvising luminary Eddie Prevost (as well as with Wade Matthews during Bernal's studies in Puebla); cellist Natalia Pérez Turner spent time in London as well as Pittsburgh, Pennsylvania; European-born violist Alexander Bruck is the son of new music guitarist Wilhelm Bruck; well-traveled Misha Marks (guitar and baritone horn) comes from New Zealand. Other members include Carlos Alegre (violin), Ramón del Buey (bass clarinet), and Fernando Vigueras (guitar and self-made instruments). The ensemble still performs today.
27. Adnán Márquez Borbón (saxophone/sound art) is also influential from this generation. Raised in Ensenada, Borbón holds a bachelor's degree from San Diego State University and a PhD from the Sonic Arts Research Center at Queen's University in Belfast, Ireland (2013). He currently teaches at UABC Ensenada and has collaborated at various places and times with Terrazas, Trujillo, and others.
28. La Semana Internacional de Improvisación began in 2014. Today it's one of the longest-running international improvised music festivals in Mexico. Trujillo also took over the Festival Internacional de Jazz, which Rosas had organized for years.
29. Díaz's contemporary music class, Ensamble de Música Contemporánea, began in 2008 at UABC.
30. Díaz de Cossio performed with the OBC on and off since her bachelor's degree began.
31. Ana Luisa Díaz de Cossio Sánchez studied from 2011–16 and Rocío Díaz de Cossio Sánchez started a few years later, from 2013–18.
32. Richards is Associate Professor of Music at UCSD.
33. This is Terrazas' Ensenada-based jazz/improvisation band Sea Quintet", with Iván Trujillo (trumpet), Edwin Montes (guitar), José Solares (saxophones), José Luis Rodríguez (double bass), and Abraham Lizardo (drums).
34. This is the Museo Histórico Regional in Ensenada.
35. Banda is a regional Mexican music typically performed by brass and percussion instruments with clear influences from European marching bands. Hussong's

(est. 1892) is Ensenada's oldest cantina, an often-rowdy site with peanut-shell strewn floors, roving *norteño* bands, and cheap drinks.

36. These were two selections from Oliveros' *Meditations for Orchestra* (1997).
37. The Verbena is a popular annual wine festival, free and open to the public every summer, in the heart of downtown at the old Santo Tomás wine processing facility. Bodegas de Santo Tomás has operated in Ensenada since 1888, very much part of the city's collective memory.
38. Amy Cimini is Assistant Professor of Music at UCSD.
39. Mexican composer Ignacio Baca Lobera came to the 2019 Festival de Música Nueva Ensenada in fulfillment of one such government grant community service requirement.
40. These were Pauline Oliveros, Kaija Saariaho, Martinez Lira, and Frida de la Sota (b. Ensenada, 1986).
41. Escobar is based in LA. The others (except Zazueta, who now attends UCSD but lived previously in Tijuana) are all currently San Diego-based. Mexico-based guest artists/clinicians included José Manuel Alcántara, Ignacio Baca Lobera, Miguel Ángel Cuevas, Álvaro Díaz, Ximena González, Carlos Rosas, and Ernesto Rosas.
42. Javier (Javi) Martínez owns Boules, a French-inspired restaurant in downtown Ensenada. His brother, David Martínez, owns Muelle 3, another fusion restaurant downtown. David studied composition in Mexico City alongside Álvaro Diaz, completed a master's degree in composition in Paris, and continues to perform in the Ensenada-based electro-acoustic improvisation band Decer with Kathia Rudametkin, Matt Lamkin (formerly of the LA-based rock group Soft Pack), and Sebastian Denigri. Here we'd like to recognize multiple ways of understanding "experimentalist" musical practice in Ensenada, acknowledging, for example, alt-pop and prog-rock groups Meltí, Childs, Dylan Brown's"Peymar, or electronic musician Murcof, who grew up in Ensenada.
43. This festival began in April 2012. For more information, find Festival Nativa on Facebook.

References

Bonifaz de Novelo, M. E. (1984, Winter). "Ensenada: Its Background, Founding, and Early Development". *San Diego Historical Society Quarterly*, 30(1). 15–26.

Nordhoff, C. (1888). *Peninsular California: Some Account of the Climate, Soil Productions, and Present Condition Chiefly of the Northern Half of Lower California.* New York: Harper.

Pauline Oliveros, "Four Meditations for Orchestra" (1997). www.paulineoliveros.us/ comssisions.html (Accessed: March 13, 2020).

Rivera, A. G. Q. (1998). *Salsa, sabor y control! sociología de la música "tropical".* México: Siglo XXI.

Stern, N. B. (1973). *Baja California: Jewish Refuge and Homeland* (No. 32). Los Angeles: Dawson's Book Shop.

Wade, P. (2000). *Music, Race, and Nation: Música Tropical in Colombia.* Chicago: University of Chicago Press.

Walker, L. E. (2013). *Waking from the Dream: Mexico's Middle Classes After 1968.* Stanford: Stanford University Press.

Zolov, E. (1999). *Refried Elvis: The Rise of the Mexican Counterculture.* Berkeley, Los Angeles, and London: University of California Press.

5 Sound Migration

Repatriation of Mexican Piano Music: A Case Study on *Three Short Piano Pieces* by Samuel Zyman

Turcios Ruiz
(English translation by Cristina Bojórquez)

Introduction

This text addresses, from the perspective of the interpreter, the appropriation of the work *Three Short Piano Pieces* by the Mexican composer Samuel Zyman through its study and further recording. These pieces were included in the independent CD called *Microcosmos, Miniaturas y micropiezas mexicanas para piano*—recorded by the author—which includes solo pieces for piano composed by Mexican composers of the 20th and 21st centuries.

Here I introduce a context that allows us to appreciate the circumstances surrounding the creation of the work *Three Short Piano Pieces*. From a subjective reading, a panorama is approached from different angles: the migration of Zyman; the influences that shaped his music; the analysis of the piece, considering briefly his work as a whole, particularly that of piano; and a personal insight in the light of concepts like influence, identity, style, and the transnational factor in the creative process. At the same time, I freely propose the notions of *sound migration* and *musical repatriation* within the scope of the aforementioned recording.

Background

The history of the cultural relations between Mexico and the United States has been forged from the exchange of ideas and people between the two countries and comprises a long series of moments of convergence and divergence that can be tracked back to Mexico's colonial period. From the 19th century, after Mexico obtained its independence from Spain, the relation with its neighbor to the north has occurred in a hazardous dynamic in which migration has brought ambivalent consequences to both countries. This can be observed in light of the events that implied major changes in the social and political organization of the country. The effects of the Mexican revolution that started in 1910, which left the nation in a state of crisis in different fields, forced an economic, political, social, and cultural reconstruction. The liberal momentum that occurred in the governments of presidents Juárez and Díaz during the 19th century was slowed down after the Revolution, and the premise for the governments that emerged from this rebellion was to find a path towards "a new sense of national identity . . . as the foundation for modernization".[1] As a consequence, during the first half of the 20th century a nationalistic trend pervaded the creation of institutions, as well as social and artistic movements, that joined the construction of such identity.

Nonetheless, reaching a modernizing development that embraces all the layers of Mexican society is a matter that even today is lagging. The living conditions of a large proportion of the population do not meet the revolutionary and post-revolutionary yearnings. As a result, a northward migratory phenomenon has taken place, particularly during the late 20th century and the 21st century. The magnitude and characteristics of this migration can be viewed as a Mexican diaspora[2] with strands expressed by groups of diverse social and cultural backgrounds, whose differences portray the Mexican cultural melting pot. These groups have created strategies to get integrated into North American society, which are a testimony to what belongs to them as part of their roots, and what is foreign but can be taken to build a new identity. This process can convey a syncretism that involves aspects such as language, food, dressing style, education, political and religious ideologies, as well as the sphere of creativity expressed through art.

Although the migration of Mexicans into the United States has been motivated mainly by an unbalance of development and opportunities related to economic growth,[3] in the art sphere many instances can be explained as an aspiration to find proper means to achieve creative goals. In this way we can track an exchange between Mexican musicians and American institutions from the first half of the 20th century, when composers like Silvestre Revueltas chose to move to the United States to pursue their education and creative dreams in an environment that the Mexican institutions could not provide.[4] This displacement of composers, interpreters, researchers, and professors into American universities and institutions resulted from the lagging caused by military, political, and social conflicts that Mexico experienced during the 19th century and the first two decades of the 20th century. This lagging hampered the development of musical proposals of composers like José Mariano Elízaga, who, along with other musicians of Mexico's independence and post-revolutionary periods, tried to overcome what had been achieved during the Spanish colony while remaining in Mexico.[5] Thus, after years of turmoil and political instability, a number of artists emigrated to the United States as they saw it as a neighboring and approachable place to develop their talents and nurture their musical yearnings.

Even though Revueltas' momentary relocation to the United States stands out, during the second half of the past century several of the most distinguished Mexican composers immigrated to the United States—perhaps not on a permanent basis—to either study or collaborate with their colleagues in the north. Composers like Blas Galindo, Joaquín Gutiérrez Heras, Leonardo Velázquez, Manuel de Elías, Manuel Enríquez, Julio Estrada, Javier Álvarez, Mariana Villanueva, and Daniel Catán, just to mention a few, have spent time studying or working in the United States.[6] The same can be said of interpreters, researchers, and professors. The case of Samuel Zyman is emblematic at the end of the 20th century, since his immigration and adaptation to North American society totals 38 years already. He is an example of an integration that has not implied a disassociation with his homeland.

A Biographical and Musical Outline of Samuel Zyman

Samuel Zyman was born in a Jewish family in 1956 in Mexico City. He began his musical education at a very young age, studying piano and accordion with Martín García and Guillermo López Hinojosa, respectively. The latter suggested he should study piano with Héctor Jaramillo—by that time first flute at UNAM Philharmonic Orchestra (OFUNAM)—who turned out to be a great influence for Zyman as he encouraged him to explore composition and piano improvisation. Later on, the composer furthered his piano studies with the jazz musician Juan José Calatayud and was enrolled in the National Conservatory of Music.[7]

At the same time, Samuel studied medicine at the National Autonomous University of Mexico. He attended medical school and completed his courses, although he has not practiced medicine so far. In the Conservatory, Samuel studied piano with María Teresa Castrillón, composition with Mario Lavista, and theory with Francisco Savín. He also studied conducting with Eduardo Díazmuñoz at the music school *Vida y Movimiento*, and composition with Humberto Hernández Medrano in his workshop of Polyphonic Studies.[8] In 1981, Samuel traveled to New York to study with Stanley Wolfe, who trained him to enter the Juilliard postgraduate school where he completed his master and doctorate studies under the guidance of Roger Sessions and David Diamond. In 1987, he became a Juilliard professor in the Department of Musical Theory and Analysis, and since then combines his work as a scholar with his creative endeavor as a composer.[9]

An Overview of Samuel Zyman's Work

The music of Samuel Zyman is comprised to the present of 70 works of various genres, among which we can find pieces for solo piano, guitar, orchestra—including two symphonies—symphonic band, choir and orchestra, as well as trios for violin, cello, and piano, and songs for voice with piano or guitar accompaniment. Also, there is an octet for trombones, a quintet for accordion and string quartet, one more for guitar and string quartet, and one for winds, strings, and piano, sonatas for instrumental duos (flute and piano, violin and piano, cello and piano, viola and piano), 11 concerts for soloist and orchestra, and music for films.[10]

His works have been performed in several countries in Europe, Latin America, and Oceania. Some of them have premiered in places like Carnegie Hall, Alice Tully Hall, and Merkin Concert Hall in the United States, as well as the Palace of Fine Arts in Mexico. Renowned musicians from Mexico and other countries have recorded his music for labels like Urtext, Digital Classics, EMI, Sony, Naxos, Island Records, and Quindecim, just to mention a few. Pieces like *Sonata for Flute and Piano*, which has become a piece of international relevance; *Encuentros*, an orchestral work with a Mexican nationalistic spirit; or *Two Motions in One Movement*, for solo piano, have also gained recognition among scholars and the general public.[11]

National Identity and Signature Style

How can our national identity condition the adoption and creation of a personal musical style? Can the musical style tell us something about the sense of national identity of its creator? Is it still possible to speak about a national identity when it comes to the musical creation of Mexican composers? These and other questions about musical creation become more relevant when the artist migrates to a place that is culturally foreign to some degree. The contemporary world allows us to communicate easily with other places and cultures, and that can generate a sensation of proximity and understanding. However, the confrontation with a surrounding that is different from ours can be challenging enough to make us reconfigure our own identity so we can express its essence and still get adjusted to the social and cultural demands of our environment. Fixed ideas that are usually understood from outside, such as national identity, are challenged in contexts where elements of diverse cultural origins come together.

From the creative point of view, defining what may be considered as national in the contemporary world asks us to take distance from notions of identity and nation based on political definitions that defend territoriality as decisive in the configuration of the national and personal identities. This vision, which sees nations as confined spaces within a geographical and legal territory, cannot explain many of the phenomena that occur today in terms of the construction of a personal identity. In a world as interconnected as the one we live in, such events tend to erase the borders that, because they were built artificially, force the states to keep a national identity through various strategies, among which the cultural policies play a pivotal role.[12]

For example, during the first decades of the 20th century, the Mexican state promoted the creation of a musical nationalism that brought together the ideas of many composers who worked on the construction of a "signature sound" that belonged to the country. This sound had different approaches with the works of Manuel M. Ponce, Silvestre Revueltas, Carlos Chávez, and José Rolón, just to mention a few. That trend led to an ideological construction that conditioned the perception of the individual styles and defined what could effectively be considered as a Mexican nationalistic style, that is, what included itself in that center, as opposed to what stayed in the periphery and was excluded.[13]

Talking about the musical style out of the framework of the prevailing ideologies is paramount to glimpse its significance and to discern the features that define both the individual and the collective. This leads us to question the musical paradigms that traditionally refer to what may be considered as national, since today diversity and multiculturalism are common in societies.[14] Contrary to an undifferentiated vision, which somehow seems to conceive the national identity as a static element without any dynamism, the phenomenon of diasporas has put on the table issues like hybridization, transnationalism, post-nationalism, and transculturation, subjects which can also encompass the field of music. Thus, according to Alejandro L. Madrid, the music composition process might be understood as an act of transculturation that implies cultural and social transformations.[15] In music, the construction of stylistic languages is carried out through processes that integrate elements from diverse cultural environments, and that is why the notion of "influence" lies underneath a large portion of the explorations in the development of western music. "Influence" for us also points towards the notion of migration of sound ideas.

Regarding Samuel Zyman's compositional style, there are elements we can trace back to different authors and periods. Although some describe him as a neo-romantic, a term which he has not dismissed,[16] this acceptance imposes on him an imprint of limited outreach. Even if his music is not tonal, at least not in the sense of the 19th-century music, Zyman's work gravitates between tonality and modality, with elements like the use of certain extended chords and sonorities that avoid making a clear reference to the major/minor systems. Likewise, some constructive features in his melodies reinforce this perception, although we can also say that certain works flow freely between tonality and atonality. As Samuel is a Mexican of Jewish ancestry, it could be assumed that he has been in touch with Mexican and Jewish music. However, he has also had close contact with the music of European canonical composers and with the music of the United States since his early childhood. Thus, his works portray influences that come especially from Latin American music, including folklore, as well as jazz, Jewish and Spanish music.[17]

In Zyman's own words, it is not possible to determine which composers, and to what degree, have influenced his musical work. He admits an influence in his work through his personal taste for the music of composers such as Bach, Schumann, Chopin, Copland, Bartók, Hindemith, and, among others, Prokofiev. This can be appreciated with accuracy in different ways. For instance, the orchestration of his *Concert for Flute and Small Orchestra* and the use of long notes in the *Sonata for Flute and Piano* reminds us of Mozart. On the other hand, a reminiscence of Prokofiev is distinguished in some of his pieces for piano by how their texture and rhythm articulate. Beethoven's use of cyclical elements is another reference for Zyman.[18] Also, an ancient air in some of the passages of the *Concert for Harp and Flute* may recall Debussy. Generally speaking, his style brings us echoes of the first stages of modernism for the use of forms and composition strategies of other times, because when drawing upon tradition, in opposition to the *avant-garde*, he does not pretend to hide the influences that nurture his work.

North American music has also played a role in his activity as a composer. The author acknowledges David Diamond as an important influence, particularly in terms of the tradition of the North American symphony. According to Siegel, the use of certain elements to create certain modal-tonal ambiguity, such as perfect fifths, brings him close to Copland, and his accessible style to Lowell Lieberman and John Harbison.[19] An interesting aspect of his whole work is that shows diverse sonorous worlds in a way similar to that of Manuel M. Ponce, approaching composition without prejudice from different strands, thus creating a consequent personal style which considers as important his ear, as well as that of his audience.

Works for Piano

So far, the music for solo piano this Mexican composer has written is comprised of five works. The house Theodore Presser Company has published three of them: *Two Motions in One Movement*, *Variations on an Original Theme*, and *Restless*. The other two works, still unpublished, are *Dance for Piano* and *Three Short Piano Pieces*. Zyman composed these works during the time he has lived in New York. *Three Short Piano Pieces* was written between 1981 and 1982, and his latest work for the instrument, *Restless*, was created for the pianist Zhenni Li and premiered in 2018.[20] On the whole, his music for piano features a distinctly rhythmic character that places it in a peculiar spot among its complete production. The conception of the piano as a percussion instrument and a rhythmic sense governed by a relentless forward thrust are some of the essential components of these pieces.

In these works, Zyman moves away from the neo-romantic style his output has been identified with. In the author's own words, according to

Dousa, his music has a clear influence from Prokofiev, Bartók, Impressionism, and jazz.[21]

Three Short Piano Pieces[22]

This work belongs to the period when Zyman traveled to New York to pursue postgraduate composition studies in Juilliard.[23] He composed the series shortly after his arrival at the institution, and Zyman considers it one of his first "serious" compositions. The author himself told me he dedicated his work to the Argentinean pianist Mirian Conti, who made its premiere during a concert for students at Juilliard. This three-piece collection has not been played again in the United States and is still waiting for its public debut in Mexico.[24]

The work has a modern sonority, which somehow reflects Zyman's intention to show a voice closer to the contemporary composers he used to listen back then.[25] It is also the author's first work for piano and already features some of the components that would become essential for the rest of his music for the instrument: a syncopated rhythm with sharp accentuations and changes of meter, as well as motive truncation, relentless impulse moving forward, use of contrasts between sections, harmonies sustained by fourths and fifths, cyclical elements, and a blend of harmonic components that refer to tonal and atonal sonorous worlds.

Allegro animato

This piece (Figure 5.1) is characterized by a vigorous rhythmic impulse that manifests through notorious accents and meter changes. We could say that rhythm is the main element that builds it up from two contrasting themes. The general structure evokes some features of the sonata because of the presence of two ideas that come in different harmonic regions, plus a section that is similar to a development. The general character reminds us of Bartók and Prokofiev for the percussive conception of the instrument, the texture, and also because of the intervallic and rhythmic construction of the motives. The texture is homophonic and features two strategies for accompanying each of the thematic ideas. The harmony is atonal with free use of chromaticism, which we can appreciate within each idea and in the sequences featured in different transpositions.

The first idea (a) is articulated with sixteenths and eights motives, contouring a melodic sequence based on melodic jumps: perfect and augmented fourths and fifths; fifths, sixths; and unison octaves. This idea also shows a chord accompaniment that punctuates the accents of the melody. The second idea (b) seems to result from the end of the first one and builds-up through a motive of sixteenths that starts repeating one same note persistently and then

1.1   Fragment of first thematic idea (a)

1.2   Fragment of second thematic idea (b)

1.3   Overlap between thematic ideas a and b

Figure 5.1 Initial Fragments of the First Thematic Idea (1.1, measures 1–3), Second Thematic Idea (1.2, measures 20–22), and How They Overlap (1.3, measures 43–46)

features a melodic descent with small intervals with changes of direction. Here, the accompaniment is generated through wide melodic intervals (fifths and sixths), creating ascending patterns with a rhythmic organization that resembles an ostinato that for moments breaks up the meter.

The character of the first idea is aggressive and opposed to the second idea, whose nature is calmer. However, the rhythmic design of the two ideas contributes to the sense of relentless forward motion. As if it were a struggle, the tension is built and increased until the end by overlapping the two ideas. Finally, the initial idea is partially evoked for closing the movement with energy, as if it were then the winning argument.

Andante tranquillo e poco rubato

The second piece (Figure 5.2) works in the fashion of the central movements of classical period's sonatas. The tempo is slow and the general character is strongly suggestive. An intimate, perhaps nostalgic, atmosphere seems to arise from the lyricism of the melodic lines and the harmonic scope that at times may reminds us of jazz. This work is structured in five sections that contrast at the expressive level through changes in the texture, tempo, dynamic, and profile of the melody.

The first section shows a jazz-like melody accompanied by freely interrelated chords sustained by a chromatic discourse, which is a feature that pervades the entire piece. The texture is homophonic and its sound arrangement seems to be compact, even though the registry fluctuates between the middle, lower, and higher notes of the instrument. The second section plays with an ornate melodic pattern in the high notes that is imitated in the lower notes. Here, the accompaniment uses the motives of fifth and sixth of the lower section of the previous piece (refer to Figure 5.1, examples 1.2 and 1.3). The rhythm of these motives also recalls some of the motives used in the initial theme from the *Allegro animato*.

The third section, *agitato*, stands out for using three sound strata: octaves in the lower range, the accompaniment motive previously mentioned now presented with harmonic intervals of fourths and fifths in the middle stratum, and a melodic line reinforced in octaves with an interspersed fourth. The harmonic handling makes a slight reference to the harmonies with fourths of McCoy Tyner's music, because of the sonorities formed by the interaction between the octaves of the bass and both the central and upper strata.[26]

The fourth section expresses a polyphonic game between two chromatic voices that move in contrary motion in the right hand. This is sustained by a harmonic construction where once more we find fourth and fifth intervals, sometimes in arpeggiated figures, and other times in chords. Again, the echo of the first piece returns with the discreet presence of a rhythmic motive coming back from the initial theme as a gesture that challenges our memory.

The last part recapitulates the theme of the first section, adding a comment that forecasts the conclusion with five-note chords and a quote of the motive of the accompaniment of the second section. Finally, a coda that is a remembrance of the initial theme closes the piece with a gesture that emphasizes its insightful, perhaps nocturnal essence.

2.1 Jazzy character in melody

2.2

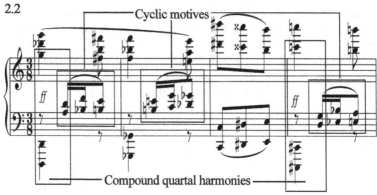

2.3 Motive derived form   Contrapuntal chromatic
first piece   passage

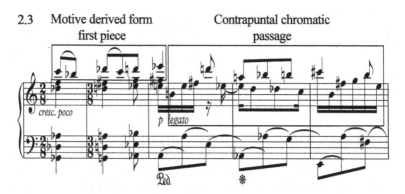

Figure 5.2 Jazzy Character in the Melody (2.1, measures 1–3); Presence of Cycli-
cal Elements (2.2, Measures 15–18); Rhythmic Motive Derived From the
First Piece (2.3, measures 36–38); Contrapuntal Elements in a Chromatic
Atmosphere (2.3, measures 38–40)

Allegro con anima

The last piece of the series (Figure 5.3) is written almost entirely in a two-voices polyphonic texture. Excluding the finale, a sort of coda with the lower voice duplicated in octaves and the upper voice moving in arpeggio figurations, the rest of the piece seems to be inspired by Bach's inventions and symphonies for two and three voices. The rhythm resembles that of a dance for its ternary meter, its motives with repeated notes, and an articulation in the style of the baroque dances. The symphony in G minor BWV 797 of the German composer might be quoted for the resemblance of some of the rhythmic motives and for the way the counterpoint is intertwined between the two voices. Also similar to the dances of the baroque, this piece manifests a general structure in two sections, although here Zyman adds a coda (A A' - Coda). In this sense, the most notorious difference is that the second section integrates with an almost whole repetition of A, but after two thirds of the piece, a *segno* brings the music to a different harmonic region that then flows to the coda.

In this piece, we can also observe the use of compositional strategies related to cycles: The motive the theme starts with seems to come from the first motive of the piece that starts the series. The only difference is that it

Figure 5.3 Contrapuntal Strategies: Imitative Contrapuntal Texture (3.1, measures 1–5); Melodic Inversion of Initial Motive (3.2, measures 24–29)

is inverted and with some differences in the intervals (refer to Figure 5.1, example 1.1). As opposed to the preceding numbers, the thematic material is scarce, as it could be assumed regarding its stylistic lineage. Zyman recurs to contrapuntal strategies typical of Bach's polyphonic music to intertwine this piece's texture. Thus, here we also find resources such as the imitation and inversion of motives. In this way, the musical discourse is built freely with a sort of dialogue in which both voices let us hear the theme at different moments, presented mostly in transpositions at an interval of fifth. Even if the piece is atonal, the arpeggios and resounding octaves of the coda make us recall for an instant the tonal music of the past.

Sound Migration and Musical Repatriation: A Final Thought

The process of knowing, studying, interpreting, and recording the work *Three Short Piano Pieces* signified the discovery of an interesting musical corpus that portrays a profile consequent with the origins and personal history of its creator. The musical style of Samuel Zyman, that is to say, his musical identity, manifests an accumulation of experiences that refer to the sounds of nationalism that migrated along with him, as well as to models that range from baroque music to the first half of the 20th century. The evocation of homeland and other musical traditions in Zyman's music seems the most capable means to connect territories that might otherwise remain isolated. This evocation, far from being just a simple influence, plays an essential role in expressing an identity that this author does not deny.

Even when we can perceive an air of romanticism in his whole output, to the extent that he has been given the adjective of neo-romantic, his piano music seems to escape from this general description. It might be rather considered as neo-modernist.

Three Short Piano Pieces is an honest and personal portrayal of Zyman's music-making. Therefore, the first recording of the piece, along with this chapter, are offered as the first bridge to communicate, and rather "repatriate", a work written by a Mexican composer in a foreign land.

Notes

1. Madrid (2008), p. 9.
2. See Rinderle (2005).
3. *Ibid.*, p. 297.
4. Early in the 20th century, Manuel M. Ponce wrote in an unpublished letter to his brother José Braulio saying that in Mexico the teaching of counterpoint used to be neglected. This commentary was made in the scope of his travel to Italy with the intention of studying with Enrico Bossi (Ponce 1905, p. 4.). Furthermore,

Samuel Zyman expressed in a 2007 interview that he considered it advantageous to study at Juilliard, and recommended to do so if possible. This, despite the fact that he also considers that in Mexico it is possible nowadays to have a good education as a composer. Nevertheless, his commentary suggests that North American institutions allow access to opportunities that are difficult to have in Mexico. Fey Berman's interview with the composer. www.letraslibres.com/mexico/sube-sam-te-ayudo-entrevista-samuel-zyman?page=full (Accessed: November 24, 2019).

5. Carmona (1984), pp. 20, 31.
6. In her book *La composición en México en el siglo XX* (1996), Yolanda Moreno Rivas offers brief biographical sketches that allow to observe the interchange that some of the most relevant Mexican composers have had with the United States during their professional career.
7. Biographical information about Zyman is scarce and is collected in some brief writings. The broadest and—in the author's opinion—with greater insight and precision in the information, are two interviews with the composer: one from 1999 on the occasion of a doctoral thesis by Merrie R. Siegel; and the other of 2012, also coming from a doctoral thesis by Nayeli Dousa.
8. In the style of the famous French pedagogue Nadia Boulanger, Humberto Hernández Medrano taught private lessons at his home where, over 30 years, other Mexican musicians and composers were also trained; among them were Mariana Villanueva, Ana Lara, Alejandro Corona, and Miguel Salmón del Real. See Pareyón (2006), p. 486.
9. Dousa (2013), pp. 17–23.
10. Theodore Presser Company Music Publisher and Distributor, "Samuel Zyman", www.presser.com/samuel-zyman?p=2#composer-tabs_content_1 (Accessed: November 9, 2019).
11. *Ibid.*
12. In her paper "Identity, Space and the Media: Thinking through Diaspora" (2010), Myria Georgiou affirms that "Territoriality is indeed anachronistic but remains deeply rooted in political conceptualisations of identity; this is why formal citizenship remains (or has become reinvented to be) property of those having long and usually rooted into territory rights", p. 18.
13. The case of composer Julián Carrillo demonstrates this trend during the first part of the last century. See Madrid (2003), p. 1.
14. According to Susan Rinderle:

> Displacement that leads to a diasporic condition is physical but can also be cultural. . . . Cultural dislocation leads to hybridity. . . . This. . . *challenges the concept of the discrete nation state.*
> (Rinderle, *op. cit.*, p. 297, italics added)

In the same way, Corona and Madrid (2008, p. 3) affirm that currently

> new approaches understand the nation-State as an "imagined community" whose existence is based upon the discursive homogenization of the diverse groups it seeks to represent [emphasizing] that culture and the people who produce it, consume it, and identify with it continuously move through the borders of the nation-State via a wide range of technologies.

15. Madrid, *op. cit.*, p. 5.
16. See Fey Berman's interview with the composer, *op. cit.*

17. Ruiz (2017), p. 18.
18. Siegel (2000), pp. 10, 11, 33.
19. *Ibid.*, pp. 32, 94.
20. The video of the premiere is accessible on YouTube.
21. Dousa, *op. cit.*, p. 30.
22. In part, this section is based on the notes published in the booklet of the afore-mentioned recording. Ruiz, *op. cit.*, p. 18.
23. This series of three pieces is designated in different ways in various writings. Siegel lists it as *Three Movements for Piano* and Dousa as *Three Solo Piano Pieces*. However, the composer wrote with pencil the name *Tres piezas cortas para piano* (*Three Short Piano Pieces*) on the first page of the manuscript's photocopy, which he gave me to study. During the transcription I made of the score, in order to be able to read it more comfortably (the drawings of the musical examples in this section are my own), I adopted the English translation of the title (*Three Short Piano Pieces*), considering that to have the digital score with the title in English would be more useful for him, as he resides in New York. Then, due to an oversight because I got used to studying the music from the transcribed version, the title was translated from English to Spanish as *Tres piezas breves para piano*, which is how it appears in the list of works of the recording mentioned in the introduction of this text. Regarding the year of composition, an annotation made with pencil by the composer himself on the photocopy of the manuscript lets us read: ca. 1982. However, Dousa mentions the year 1981. See Siegel, *op. cit.*, p. 95; Dousa, *op. cit.*, p. 6; and Ruiz, *op. cit.*, pp. 1, 18.
24. Chat with the composer via Facebook Messenger, dated November 1, 2017.
25. Dousa, *op. cit.*, p. 24.
26. In her study, Dousa mentions that this handling of harmony is a common feature in other piano works by Zyman. See Dousa, *op. cit.*, pp. 54–55.

References

Carmona, G. (1984). "La música en México durante la Independencia (1822–1839)". In *La música de México* (Vol. 3, ed. Julio Estrada). México: Universidad Nacional Autónoma de México. 212.

Corona, I., & Madrid, A.L. (2008). "Introduction: The Postnational Turn in Music Scholarship and Music Marketing". In *Postnational Musical Identities: Cultural Production, Distribution and Consumption in a Globalized Scenario* [co-edit with Ignacio Corona]. Lanham: Lexington Books. 3.

Dousa, N. (2013). *The Piano Works of a Contemporary Mexican Expatriate: Samuel Zyman's Two Motions in One Movement and Variations on an Original Theme*, Doctoral Thesis, The University of Arizona. 110.

Georgiu, M. (2010). "Identity, Space and the Media: Thinking Through Diaspora". *Revue européenne des migrations internationales*, 26(1). 17–35. Université de Poitiers.

Madrid, A. L. (2003). *Transculturación, performatividad e identidad en la Sinfonía No. 1 de Julián Carrillo*. Columbus: Universidad Estatal de Ohio. 7.

———. (2008). *Sounds of the Modern Nation*. Philadelphia, PA: Temple University Press. 210.

Moreno Rivas, Y. (1996). *La composición en México en el siglo XX.* Mexico: CONA-CULTA. 383.

Pareyón, G. (2006). *Diccionario Enciclopédico de Música en México* (Tomo 1). Mexico: Universidad Panamericana. 555.

Ponce, M. M. (1905). Letter of Manuel M. Ponce to his brother José Braulio Ponce. Bologna, Italy, 19 January. Acervo Ponce, Biblioteca de las Artes, Centro Nacional de las Artes, México. 4.

Rinderle, S. (2005). "The Mexican Diaspora: A Critical Examination of Signifiers". *Journal of Communication Inquiry,* 29. 294–316.

Ruiz, T. (2017). "Tres piezas breves para piano". In *Microcosmos, Miniaturas y micropiezas mexicanas para piano.* Recording booklet. Mexico: Programa de Estímulo a la Creación y Desarrollo Artístico Morelos (PECDA). 23.

Siegel, M. R. (2000). *Samuel Zyman's Concerto for Flute and Small Orquestra and Sonata for Flute and Piano,* Doctoral Thesis, Rice University, Houston, TX. 111.

6 Borderline Crossings

The New Mexican Orchestra

Mauricio Rodríguez

In May 1940, the Museum of Contemporary Art in New York offered a series of concerts to represent different periods of Mexican music. For the occasion, Carlos Chávez presented his *Xochipilli-Macuilxóchitl*, a work in which he used replicas of pre-Hispanic instruments with the intention, according to the composer, to capture the essence of the sonorities characterized in pre-Columbian music (Stevenson, 1954: 1). These concerts had a very positive reception from the American public, among other things, due to the "unexpected rarity of primitive sonorities . . . show(ing) the least traces of European influence" (Stevenson, 1954: 3). The MoMA concerts, which also included other works by Chávez and music by his students and followers, would represent the last artistic activities carried out by Chávez conducting his very original and innovative Mexican Orchestra, a group that he himself formed at the outset of the 1930s.

The cultural environment that consolidated the Mexican Orchestra implied one of the most effervescent cultural periods in Mexico (Malmström, 1977), a time that would give rise to the generic idea of a *Mexican Music School*, Chávez himself being the main figure of this nationalist movement (Moreno Rivas, 1994: 43). The post-revolutionary era of the 1920s required a cultural program that, on the one hand, would mitigate the economic and social stress left by the revolution, and that at the same time would serve as a project to create a "new and equitable Nation". In his position as a cultural strategist leading the Department of Fine Arts, Chávez imprinted a socialist character in his musical policy, and to get closer to the people and distance himself from the "decadent European culture" (Moreno Rivas, 1989: 135), he found indigenous music and pre-Cortesian Mexican art as the seemingly inexhaustible sources to create a unique and authentically Mexican music identity (Sturman, 2015: 46).

The Mexican Orchestra and its presentations at the MoMA were part of Chávez's great project to internationalize (essentially towards the US) a new and vitalized Mexican musical art inspired by an (imagined) Aztecan renaissance. With his Mexican Orchestra, Chávez sought to overcome and leave aside the image of the Orquesta Típica Mexicana, whose popularity in the

Figure 6.1 Pasatono Orquesta Mexicana

United States since the late 19th century was the cultural emblem to convey the ideal of social and economic stability of an evolving Mexico.

The internationalization of nationalist music by Chávez and his followers continued in the United States thanks to other opportunities that the composer had conducting in the American union; however, his original Mexican Orchestra fell into a deep hibernation of eight decades before boldly resurfacing again.

In 2013, precisely 80 years after the creation of Chávez's Mexican Orchestra, a group of ethnomusicologists led by Ruben Luengas reconstituted the orchestra under the support of Instrumenta Oaxaca International Festival. The new POM: Pasatono Mexican Orchestra (Figure 6.1) is a unique ensemble fully committed to continue Chávez's legacy to bridge the worlds of concert (academic) and folk music. However, unlike Chávez's original idea, the new Mexican Orchestra is not only a musical project with a strong social impact (as discussed in the following), but it is a solid space for ethnomusicological research, an educational "hub", and an ensemble that welcomes innovative and experimental explorations.

Mexican Orchestra in Oaxaca and the US

POM was initially conformed as an ensemble dedicated to rescuing and performing traditional Oaxacan music, especially that of the Mixtec region. POM is partly constituted by musicians whose training is strongly rooted on folk tradition, insiders of the musical tradition they study and practice. Their music education, received on self-organized community schools, or "Escolas", allows these musicians "to speak" a vernacular musical language they naturally possess, a language that needs no musicological translation for the traditional repertory they play. This musical quality is essentially different from Chávez's orchestra, where academic musicians were required to perform and recreate a musical culture that was beyond their background experience.

Protective of its learning tradition, POM runs a continuous education program bringing "Escolas" to the most distant regions in Oaxaca State, educating hundreds of emerging musicians from traditionally underserved rural communities. This musical project has had a positive social impact, particularly in the rural young population who traditionally emigrate to Mexico City or to the US due to the lack of opportunities. By creating bonds and opportunities within Oaxacan communities, POM has trained emerging musicians who take root in their own communities, and if these young musicians cross to the US, they do so under their musician status, touring for performances with POM throughout the American union. POM has extensively toured in United States, becoming an original cultural ambassador of Mexican music to internationalize its repertory and bringing its music to the large Mexican community settled in the US. The orchestra has played in prestigious venues such as Lincoln Center in New York, the Kennedy Center in Washington D.C., the Smithsonian American Art Museum, the National Museum of Mexican Art, the Mexican Cultural Institute in Washington D.C., Museo del Barrio in New York City, the Getty Museum in LA, and in academic institutions such as Bard College, Oxnard College, the University of Colorado Boulder, and Stanford University, among other venues.

The new Mexican Orchestra has become an artistic music project that greatly supersedes Chávez's initial conception for an ensemble devoted to performing music by post-revolutionary composers. The inclusive programing of POM includes traditional Oaxacan music as well as the "canonic" nationalistic composers (e.g., Carlos Chávez, Silvestre Revueltas, Pablo Moncayo, Blas Galindo, and Luis Sandi, among others). POM has also commissioned and collaborated with varied contemporary performers including musicians such as Enrico Chapela and Eugenia Leon, as well as US artists such as Golem Band, Lila Downs, and Dom Flemons. With these collaborative projects, POM has presented fresh music expressions where jazz, bel-canto, folk-punk, and country music meet and hybridize with traditional Mixtec music, chilenas, polkas, and even cumbia. The flexibility of director Ruben Luengas, aiming for a contemporary reinterpretation (and not just a recuperation) of traditional Mexican music, is what inspired my collaboration with the orchestra, a collaboration that honors traditional Mexican music and its symbolisms reinterpreted in the context of contemporary, *borderline* sonic art.

New Music for the Mexican Orchestra (Rodriguez, 2018)

In 2015 I was commissioned by Instrumenta Oaxaca International Festival to compose a chamber orchestra piece for POM. With this work I wanted to reflect my position as an immigrant Mexican composer, exploring the extent to which my own personal displacement from my homeland into a foreign country has shaped my musical thinking and creative and aesthetic concerns. This work eventually became a metaphorical exploration of a transcontinental archaeoacoustics, whose inspiration is the art and symbolisms of native Mexican-American people.

When composing my work for POM I wanted to be sensitive to the mission and the specific cultural background of this group of players, so before starting the composition of my piece, I searched for and listened to several old field recordings of folk and indigenous music, such as the performances archived by the former Indigenous Mexican Institute (FONAPAS-INI, 1980); I also saw videos from different ritual practices, as documented in a series of DVDs released by the Mexican Commission for Development of Indigenous People (CDI, 2008); I studied the organology and context of the musical instruments that I planned to use, reading the comprehensive *Musical Atlas* by ethnomusicologist Guillermo Contreras (1988); and lastly, I planned a short artistic residency at Oaxaca to revive my relation with the region and to collect musical instruments and sound objects that I could use in the piece. This planned residency took place just one week before the montage and premiering of the work, so while composing the piece, I had in mind that some of the instrumental selections would be decided upon my fieldwork explorations once in Oaxaca.

The process just described reinforced my awareness to consider that writing music for this particular orchestra would not just be about composing music for it, but creating a sounding experience that would have to be framed into a larger cultural context, a context that would consider and try to capture the very nature of music meaning and music making for this specific group of performers.

Music for these performers is not just an isolated sounding artistic expression but it is often associated with extra-musical elements, such as feast, ritual, nature, and human relationships, vital concepts such as life, death, time, and so on. Therefore, music generally takes place within a larger art-form that is interdisciplinary in its essence, and that might include varied forms of cultural and artistic expression such as dance, poetry, gastronomy, environmental interactions, etc. Being aware of this ample meaning of music, I was decidedly interested in exploring forms of musical expression that would be presented in a multimodal art-form, where for instance, choreographic and scenographic actions, among other kinds of stage interventions, would be integrated as part of the musical unfold.

Historians and ethnomusicologists have suggested that the multidisciplinary nature of art-making found in some contemporary native Mexican-American art is clearly rooted into the pre-Columbian concept of *Cuicatl-Tlahtolli*, a Nahuatl idea that literally (but not completely) translates as the bi-term *Chant-Word* (León-Portilla, 1983). Cuicatl in this context means music, dance, and dramatic expression altogether, working as a single and compound art-form, while Tlahtolli refers to the literary representation of literal, figurative, and abstract thought presented in the form of narrative or prose. The Wagnerian *Gesamtkunstwerk* idea might be helpful here to understand the "synthesis of arts" concept implicit in Cuicatl-Tlahtolli, except that for the Nahuatl world there is not a preliminary distinction of different art disciplines forming a whole: it is this necessarily compound art-form what is actually conceived as *Chant* or *Poetry*.

The Cuicatl-Tlahtolli concept was the inspirational source for my own artistic project with POM. I started the pre-composition of the piece by trying to understand how the Cuicatl-Tlahtolli idea would manifest itself through the fragmented and scarce known documents from and around the pre-Hispanic era. Therefore, I studied (in a rather empirical way) different pre-Columbian codices that I accessed in digital form as they were released by their respective custodians (Gómez, 2006). Once I collected these documents, I observed their formal and structural constructions, the narrative, allegorical, and symbolic elements used, their pictorial representation techniques, their material compositions: pigments and colors, textures created by paper types (or *amatl*), the calligraphic styles employed, etc. Only then did I begin thinking how those elements could systematically translate and materialize in my own composition. One salient methodological problem out of this empiric-observational strategy is the imminent subjective risk of just creating a "personal folklore" out of a rather elaborate Nahuatl cosmogony. An imagined interpretation based on the profound Nahuatl world could be ultimately justified under the same terms much of the postmodernist "primitive compositions" are, but I consistently wanted to create something different from just an "autochthonous positivistic" work. Therefore, I had to re-evaluate my original observations and try to understand how the cultural contents and symbolisms found in those antique codices are actually expressed, embodied, and re-symbolized in current practices of native Mexican art. I worked under that approach with the hope that I could recognize, and later depict in my own work, the elements that most purely define the authentic *ethos* of what could be called a vernacular Latin American music; looking for a

Mesoamerican ethos in the present, by pondering the humanistic and aesthetic values as they are found in contemporary native art, is in accordance with what composer-musicologist Gabriel Pareyón has observed when he says: "It is urgent to study the concepts, traditions, symbolic values, and techniques of our indigenous cultures, all of them clearly undermined by our undergoing post-colonial lifestyle" (Pareyón, 2013: 6).

However, the searching for an authentic *Mexican music* inspired on the endless and heterogeneous principles of Native Mexicanity is a very controversial topic, one that I nevertheless had to address since my work for POM had to be written. The concept of Mexican Music is diffuse indeed, and over the years has had different meanings. Before the nationalistic Chávez's time, romantic composer Manuel M. Ponce coined the term *Mexican Song*, defining as such the music inspired on folk songs of mestizo (half indigenous, half European) origin. Later, and up to the first half of the 20th century, there were numerous chamber and orchestral music works written whose indigenous titles were used as a rather political gesture to denote an ideal rebirth of a pretended *New Mexican Identity*; however, most of the pieces at that time followed the aesthetics and technical molds of Western musical practices, whose formal and material strategies were imposed over the rather picturesque treatment of indigenous elements (Estrada, 1982). It has been just in recent years that contemporary Mexican composers have consistently searched for an artistic expression that thoroughly, critically, and vividly embraces the knowledge, symbology, and aesthetic values of a millenary Mexicanity that is fully recontextualized into the contemporary arena. This new musical expression is profoundly inspired and informed by current research in semiotics, linguistics, aesthetics, musicology, and archaeoacoustics around old and contemporary native Mexican art (Pareyón, 2013). These scientific disciplines are constantly providing the unified stratum from where individual artistic voices are stylistically cast: Julio Estrada, Guillermo Galindo, Roberto Morales, and Gabriel Pareyón are some among the authors that had consistently shaped an innovative musical artistry that is profoundly Mexican.

Despite the very original musical ideas that each composer of this *New Mexican Music* has contributed (Tello, 2010), the issue of writing contemporary music without undermining the folk knowledge of performers was never fully addressed before, a problem that poses its own intricacies. In trying to approach those difficulties, I followed two directions: one ideological and aesthetic, and the other technical.

The aesthetics and idiosyncrasy I observe in the artistic expression of some native Mexican art are so radical in their essence that they can be easily paired to the most experimental and innovative practices of contemporary art. For instance, in the known performing rite practiced by the Papantla Flyers from Veracruz Mexico, a group of performers literally fly to execute music while hanging upside down from ropes until they gradually reach the ground, risking their lives while descending from a 60-foot tall pole. Beyond the ritual implications of this performance, the mere fact of conceiving and bringing into reality (and not just virtually alluding to) the possibility of flying to produce music is, as I find it, a very original form of poetics. This free-mind spirit to literally embody unexpected relations with sound and music inspired different playing techniques in my own work, where I intentionally aim to create a unique idiomatic relation among players, and between the instrument/object and performer/player relationship. As an example of the playing techniques proposed in my piece, I ask the percussion players to energetically jump to beat a huge *Tarahumara* drum hanging on the middle of the stage, or require performers throwing objects (used as "sounding arrows") to hit this hanging drum from afar. Other instrumental actions might include shaking violin bows in the air to produce buzzing sounds that recall environmental acoustics, employing bird callers and tree bushes as actual musical instruments, or using a *Charrasca* (a horse jawbone) as a hard mallet to play as *forte* as possible on a *Huéhuetl* (a pre-Hispanic standing drum). Additional instrumental techniques are presented to the players to consider the factual "sensing" of their instruments before approaching them with the standard or "culturized" artistry to play them; these techniques implicitly ask for sensorial or experiential musical actions, such as rhythmically biting a tripod rattle to produce sound.

These *physiological instrumental techniques* include the performance of different and specific movements and body actions. In order to facilitate the musical performance of those physical motions, a prescriptive or tablature-like music notation was consistently used as the technical means to represent and convey those motions in written form. An iconic notation that graphically depicts the precise positions and actions carried out from specific body parts during performance allowed me to explore the musical implications of "movement as sound".

All sorts of kinetic actions, either implying global limbic movements (such as the movement of arms, head, and legs), or local motion (such as the movement of fingers, eyes, and mouth), are suggestively represented using an iconic notation.

Lastly, the iconic prescriptive notation proposed in the score was inspired in the iconography and architecture found in pre-Columbian codices. The following example of the work indicates the players "to sculpt" the notated shapes, arranging stones that were previously employed to beat huge ceramic vessels as percussion instruments. The resulting sculptures are the symbolic containers of objects with similar shapes that will be later used in the piece as musical instruments, thus suggesting the idea that music is created "as real and material" as it unfolds. These images from a fragment of my music score and the Grolier Codex show some deliberate similarities (Figures 6.2 and 6.3).

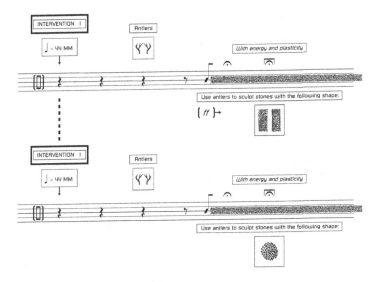

Figure 6.2 In ihiio–In iten–In itlahtol (Score Excerpt)

To appreciate the artistic result of this composition, a video recording of the premier performance of the work by Pasatono Orquesta Mexicana can be found at https://ccrma.stanford.edu/~marod/in-i.mov.

Postscript

It was right after the premiering of my work *In-ihiio-In iten-In itlahtol* when I fully realized the ultimate aesthetic and technical implications of having embarked on such a particular project. From a technical point of view, the prescriptive notation of the score has proven appropriate to realize performance situations and playing techniques that would be difficult to convey otherwise. The suggestive symbology employed throughout the score, greatly inspired by ancient Mexican iconography, set a shared common ground that effectively disinhibited POM musicians, who found in this music an "odd familiarity" when approaching its varied unconventional performance actions. Aesthetically speaking, I confirmed that the writing of music for these players ought to consider a broader artistic scope, where music is better conceived as just a part, however necessary, from a compound (holistic) art-form. Inside that complete or "Total Art" expression, it is the *self* of the player the most important part of the work.

The general note at the beginning of *In ihiio–In iten–In itlahtol*, might be just the only true contribution of the whole piece; this performance note

Figure 6.3 Grolier Codex (Fragment)

reminds players that collective creation, as opposed to individual author-ship, is surely the most distinctive and authentic landmark of universal Native Art:

> Although the notation of this score tried to be consistent and exhaus-tive, musical variations are sought to occur either as a free interpretation, re-elaboration, and/or improvisation upon the given materials with the ultimate goal of creating, "in-situ", a full re-composition of the work.

References

Comisión Nacional para el Desarrollo de los Pueblos Indígenas. (2008). *Cine Indigenista*. DVD Series. México: CDI.

Contreras-Arias, J. G. (1988). *Música. Atlas cultural de México*. México: Secretaría de Educación Pública.

Estrada, J. (1982). "Raíces y tradición en la música nueva de México y de América Latina". *Latin American Music Review*, 3(2). 188–206.

Gómez, L. A. (2006). "La documentación de la iconografía documental prehispánica". In *Revista Digital Universitaria* (Vol. 7). México: UNAM.

Instituto Nacional Indigenista. (1980). *Encuentros de música tradicional indígena*. México: FONAPAS-INI.

León-Portilla, M. (1983). "Cuícatl y Tlahtolli. Las formas de expresión en náhuatl". *Estudios de cultura náhuatl*, 16. 245.

Malmström, D. (1977). *Introducción a la música mexicana del siglo XX* (Vol. 263). México: Fondo de Cultura Económica.

Moreno Rivas, Y. (1989). *Rostros del nacionalismo en la música mexicana: un ensayo de interpretación*. México: Universidad Nacional Autónoma de México.

———. (1994). *La composición en México en el siglo XX*. México: Consejo Nacional para la Cultura y las Artes.

Pareyón, G. (2013). *El resurgimiento de lenguas e instrumentos originarios en la composición musical en México*. México: Sociedad de Geografía y Estadística del Estado de Jalisco.

Rodriguez, M. (2018). "In ihiio-In iten-In itlahtol: New Music for the Mexican Orchestra". Copyright (2018) Perspectives of New Music. Used by permission. This article first appeared in *Perspectives of New Music*, 56(1).

Stevenson, R. (1954). *Music in Mexico, a Historical Survey*. Mexico: Thomas Crowell Company.

Sturman, J. (2015). *The Course of Mexican Music*. London: Routledge.

Tello, A. (2010). *La Música en México: panorama del siglo XX*. México: Consejo Nacional para la Cultura y las Artes.

Contributors

Teresa Díaz de Cossio is a Mexican flutist and teacher, currently pursuing a DMA at the University of California, San Diego under the tutelage of Wilfrido Terrazas. Teresa's mentors include Dr. Tara Helen O'Connor, Pamela Martchev, Leopoldo Gonzalez at the Universidad, and Catherine Ransom Karoly. A former fellow of The Banff Centre, she has participated in master classes with Martin Michael Köfler, Jim Walker, Lorna McGhee, Patrick Gallois, and Ransom Wilson. In 2017, with flutist Stefanie Proulx, she started the Festival de Música Nueva, Ensenada. Teresa teaches at Universidad Autónoma de Baja California.

Álvaro G. Díaz Rodríguez is a full-time professor and researcher at the Universidad Autónoma de Baja California (UABC), Mexico. His research focuses on contemporary music, cyberculture and music, and soundscapes supported by technology. Díaz received his PhD in Musicology from the Universidad Católica Argentina. In his other activity as a performer he is a conductor of ensembles and orchestras, which involve contemporary music. His research "Visual sound mapping (SONVI). Platform for dialogue between the visual and sound, as an artistic resource for the memory of the city" received the Art, Science and Technology (ACT) grant from the National Fund for the Culture and the Arts and the Universidad Nacional Autónoma de México (2018). He is the founder and CEO of the SONVI project, which has an app and platform for the recognition and classification of soundscapes. He is the author of chapters in the books *A razón de la nostalgia* (UABC, 2006), *Sound in Motion: Cinema, Videogames, Technology and Audiences* (Cambridge Scholars Publishing, 2018), *La investigación musical en las regiones de México* (Texere, 2018), and editor of the book *Visiones Amorfas: Approaches to Art Since the 21st Century* (UABC, 2018). He has received several grants and distinctions for his career: National Fund for Culture and Arts (2010, 2015); Distinguished Citizen by the City Council of Ensenada (2011);

and University Merit (2018). He is a member of the National System of Researchers in Mexico.

Mauricio Rodríguez holds a doctor of musical arts degree in Composition from Stanford University, a master's in Sonology from the Royal Conservatory, The Hague in The Netherlands, and a bachelor's degree in composition, Piano, and Ethnomusicology from the University of Mexico (UNAM). His music is frequently played in the Americas and Europe. He has been artist in residence at the Arteles Center (Finland), University of California Santa Cruz (WACM-Workshop), International Centre for Composers (Gotland-Sweden), Xenakis Centre (France), Formations Professionnelles Royaumont (France), and Cuban Institute of Art. His research has been published by *Perspectives of New Music*, *Perspectiva Interdisciplinaria de Música* (University of Mexico), IRCAM, Stanford University, the Burgos Foundation, and *Babel Scores*. He has taught composition, music theory, and music technology at Stanford University, School of Music of Catalonia, Conservatory of Castile and Leon Spain, San José State University, San Francisco Conservatory of Music, and San José City College. He is an artistic fellow of the National Endowment for the Arts of Mexico.

Paul N. Roth is an American saxophonist, improviser/composer, radio artist, and scholar working across and in between various disciplines. He is currently pursuing a PhD in the Integrative Studies program at the University of California, San Diego. From 2011–18 he lived and worked in Berlin, Germany, where he served on the curatorial team for "ausland", one of Europe's premiere venues for experimental music and art. His work is published on SNP Records, Honor Roll Records, Hail Ants, Floating Forest, Earwash Records, AUT Records, and others.

Turcios Ruiz studied the piano at the National School of Music of UNAM. His professional interests have led him to venture into the areas of performance, musicology, music diffusion, and teaching. As a pianist, he has offered recitals of solo piano and chamber music in forums such as the Teatro Degollado, Teatro de las Artes, Sala Manuel M. Ponce, and Teatro Ocampo. Various Mexican composers have dedicated works to him that he has premiered in concert and recording. His discography includes three albums, two of them devoted to contemporary Mexican music: *Entre Cuerdas. Música mexicana para guitarra y piano*, and *Microcosmos. Miniaturas y micro-piezas mexicanas para piano*. In the field of musicology, he has collaborated on several publications dedicated to Mexican music, such as the books *La música de Conlon Nancarrow* by Kyle Gann, and *Canto Roto: Silvestre Revueltas* by Julio Estrada. He has also published in the university journal of musicology *PIM* (*Perspectiva Interdisciplinaria de Música*, UNAM), and in *Inventio* (UAEM). He is currently developing a research project on the youth stage of Mexican composer Manuel M. Ponce, which involves the preparation of a book with 57 unpublished letters and the recording of a compact disc. In the area of music programming, he is secretary of the Mexican chapter of The Ponce Project, an initiative based in Houston, which seeks to disseminate Latin American music in the United States and in Mexico. He has also made four radio series: *Mozart llama al oído* (Opus 94.5, IMER), *Música al descubierto*, *Diccionario Musical*, and *Ocho x radio* (UFM Alterna 106.1, UAEM)— the latter dedicated to Mexican concert music. He is a professor at La Salle Cuernavaca University School of Music, of which he was also Academic Coordinator. He has received various grants and scholarships from the National System of Researchers (SNI), the Government of Mexico, and the Government of the State of Morelos.

Wilfrido Terrazas is a Mexican flutist, improviser, composer, and educator, whose work finds points of convergence between notated and improvised music, and approaches collaboration and collective creation in innovative ways. He is a member of two Mexico City–based projects: the improvisers' collective Generación Espontánea, and Liminar, an experimental music ensemble; and he has performed more than 350 world premieres, written more than 50 compositions, and recorded around 30 albums. Wilfrido has presented his work all over Mexico, and in other 18 countries in Europe and the Americas. He has obtained support from the National Fund for the Culture and the Arts (FONCA) and several other Mexican institutions, and has been an artist in residence at Omi International Arts Center (Ghent, New York), Atlantic Center for the Arts (New Smyrna, Florida), and Ionion Center for the Arts and Culture (Kefalonia, Greece). Since 2014, he is co-curator of the Semana Internacional de Improvisación, a festival completely dedicated to improvised music in Ensenada, his hometown. Other current projects include *Filera* (a trio with vocalist Carmina Escobar and cellist Natalia Pérez Turner) and the Wilfrido Terrazas Sea Quintet. Recent collaborations include recording with Roscoe Mitchell (*Discussions*, Wide Hive, 2017) and playing with Angélica Castelló, Andrew Drury, Vinny Golia, Stephanie Griffin, Katt Hernandez, Lisa Mezzacappa, and Wade Matthews. In 2017, he was appointed Assistant Professor of Music at the University of California, San Diego.

Rossana Lara Velázquez is a musician, improviser, and a musicologist who specializes in electronic cultures, contemporary music, experimental scenes, and sound art in Mexico, from the perspective of anthropology, media and sound studies, and the geopolitics of art and science production in the context of Latin America. Since 2015, she is Professor of the Master and Doctorate Music Program at Universidad Nacional Autónoma de México as well as a professor of sound and media studies in private college institutions. From 2008 to 2016 she participated in the annual International Conference on Systems Research, Informatics, and Cybernetics in Baden-Baden, Germany, and has presented some of her research at the International Congress on Musical Signification, the symposium Noise in and as Music at Huddersfield University, the symposium Mapping Sound and Urban Space in the Americas at Cornell University, and at the International Conference of Live Coding, among others. In 2018 she was part of the curators crew of the Mexican sound art exhibition *Modos de oír: prácticas de arte y sonido en México*. Since 2018 she coordinates a seminar on art, science, and complexity at Centro de Ciencias de la Complejidad (UNAM).

Index

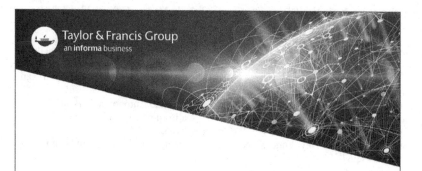

Printed in the United States
by Baker & Taylor Publisher Services